Harvard Business Review

ON

MANAGING

PEOPLE

THE HARVARD BUSINESS REVIEW PAPERBACK SERIES

The series is designed to bring today's managers and professionals the fundamental information they need to stay competitive in a fast-moving world. From the preeminent thinkers whose work has defined an entire field to the rising stars who will redefine the way we think about business, here are the leading minds and landmark ideas that have established the *Harvard Business Review* as required reading for ambitious businesspeople in organizations around the globe.

Other books in the series:

Harvard Business Review on the Business Value of IT

Harvard Business Review on Change

Harvard Business Review on Entrepreneurship

Harvard Business Review on Knowledge Management

Harvard Business Review on Leadership

Harvard Business Review on Managing Uncertainty

Harvard Business Review on Measuring Corporate Performance

Harvard Business Review on Nonprofits

Harvard Business Review on Strategies for Growth

Harvard Business Review

ON

MANAGING PEOPLE

A HARVARD BUSINESS REVIEW PAPERBACK

The *Harvard Business Review* articles in this collection are available as individual reprints. Discounts apply to quantity purchases. For information and ordering please contact Customer Service, Harvard Business School Publishing, Boston, MA 02163. Telephone: (617) 783-7500 or (800) 988-0886, 8 A.M. to 6 P.M. Eastern Time, Monday through Friday. Fax: (617) 783-7555, 24 hours a day. E-mail: custserv@hbsp.harvard.edu

Library of Congress Cataloging-in-Publication Data
Harvard business review on managing people.
        p.   cm.—(The Harvard business review paperback series)
    Includes index.
    ISBN 0-87584-907-5 (alk. paper)
    1. Personnel Management.   I. Harvard business review.
II. Series.
HF5549.H3442   1999
658.3—dc21   98-44997
                                                          CIP

The paper used in this publication meets the requirements of the American National Standard for Permanence of Paper for Printed Library Materials Z39.49-1984.

Contents

What Holds the Modern Company Together?   1
ROB GOFFEE AND GARETH JONES

Pygmalion in Management   45
J. STERLING LIVINGSTON

Six Dangerous Myths About Pay   73
JEFFREY PFEFFER

Empowerment: *The Emperor's New Clothes*   101
CHRIS ARGYRIS

Making Differences Matter: *A New Paradigm for
Managing Diversity*   121
DAVID A. THOMAS AND ROBIN J. ELY

The Alternative Workplace: *Changing Where and How
People Work*   155
MAHLON APGAR, IV

The Set-Up-to-Fail Syndrome   197
JEAN-FRANÇOIS MANZONI AND JEAN-LOUIS BARSOUX

The Necessary Art of Persuasion   227
JAY A. CONGER

About the Contributors   257

Index   261

Harvard
Business
Review

ON

MANAGING

PEOPLE

What Holds the Modern Company Together?

ROB GOFFEE AND GARETH JONES

Executive Summary

THE ORGANIZATIONAL WORLD is awash with talk of corporate culture—and for good reason. Culture has become a powerful way to hold a company together against the recent tidal wave of pressures for disintegration, such as decentralization and downsizing. But what is culture? Perhaps more important, is there one *right* culture for every organization? And if the answer is no, how can a manager change an organization's culture?

Addressing those three questions, Rob Goffee and Gareth Jones begin the article with the assertion that culture is community. Moreover, they contend, because business communities are no different from communities outside the commercial arena—such as families, schools, clubs, and villages—they can (and should) be viewed through the same lens that has illuminated the study of human organizations for nearly 150 years.

That is the lens of sociology, which divides community into two types of human relations: *sociability,* a measure of friendliness among members of a community, and *solidarity,* a measure of a community's ability to pursue shared objectives. Plotting these two dimensions against each other results in four types of business community: networked, mercenary, fragmented, and communal. None of these cultures is "the best," the authors say. In fact, each is appropriate for different business environments. In other words, managers need not advocate one cultural type over another. Instead, they must know how to assess their own culture and whether it fits the competitive situation. Only then can they consider the delicate techniques for transforming it.

THE ORGANIZATIONAL WORLD IS AWASH with talk of corporate culture—and for good reason. Culture has become a powerful way to hold a company together against a tidal wave of pressures for disintegration, such as decentralization, de-layering, and downsizing. At the same time, traditional mechanisms for integration—hierarchies and control systems, among other devices—are proving costly and ineffective.

Culture, then, is what remains to bolster a company's identity as one organization. Without culture, a company lacks values, direction, and purpose. Does that matter? For the answer, just observe any company with a strong culture—and then compare it to one without.

But what is corporate culture? Perhaps more important, is there one right culture for every organization? And if the answer is no—which we firmly believe—how can a manager change an organization's culture? Those three questions are the subject of this article.

Culture, in a word, is community. It is an outcome of how people relate to one another. Communities exist at work just as they do outside the commercial arena. Like families, villages, schools, and clubs, businesses rest on patterns of social interaction that sustain them over time or are their undoing. They are built on shared interests and mutual obligations and thrive on cooperation and friendships. It is because of the commonality of all communities that we believe a business's culture can be better understood when viewed through the same lens that has illuminated the study of human organizations for nearly 150 years.

That is the lens of sociology, which divides community into two types of distinct human relations: sociability and solidarity. Briefly, *sociability* is a measure of

Two Dimensions, Four Cultures

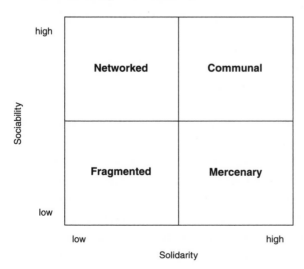

sincere friendliness among members of a community. *Solidarity* is a measure of a community's ability to pursue shared objectives quickly and effectively, regardless of personal ties. These two categories may at first seem not to capture the whole range of human behaviors, but they have stood the test of close scrutiny, in both academia and the field.

What do sociability and solidarity have to do with culture? The answer comes when you plot the dimensions against each other. The result is four types of community: networked, mercenary, fragmented, and communal. (See the matrix "Two Dimensions, Four Cultures.") None of these cultures is "the best." In fact, each is appropriate for different business environments. In other words, managers need not begin the hue and cry for one cultural type over another. Instead, they must know how to assess their own culture and whether it fits the competitive situation. Only then can they consider the delicate techniques for transforming it.

Sociability and Solidarity in Close Focus

Sociability, like the laughter that is its hallmark, often comes naturally. It is the measure of emotional, noninstrumental relations (those in which people do not see others as a means of satisfying their own ends) among individuals who regard one another as friends. Friends tend to share certain ideas, attitudes, interests, and values and usually associate on equal terms. In its pure form, sociability represents a type of social interaction that is valued for its own sake. It is frequently sustained through continuing face-to-face relations characterized by high levels of unarticulated reciprocity. Under these circumstances, there are no prearranged "deals." We help one another, we talk, we share, we laugh and cry together—with no strings attached.

In business communities, the benefits of high sociability are clear and numerous. First, most employees agree that working in such an environment is enjoyable, which helps morale and esprit de corps. Sociability also is often a boon to creativity because it fosters teamwork, sharing of information, and a spirit of openness to new ideas, and allows the freedom to express and accept out-of-the-box thinking. Sociability also creates an environment in which individuals are more likely to go beyond the formal requirements of their jobs. They work harder than is technically necessary to help their colleagues— that is, their community—look good and succeed.

But there also are drawbacks to high levels of sociability. The prevalence of friendships may allow poor performance to be tolerated. No one wants to rebuke or fire a friend. It's more comfortable to accept—and excuse— subpar performance in light of an employee's personal problems. In addition, high-sociability environments are often characterized by an exaggerated concern for consensus. That is to say, friends are often reluctant to disagree with or criticize one another. In business settings, such a tendency can easily lead to diminished debate over goals, strategies, or simply how work gets done. The result: the best *compromise* gets applied to problems, not the best *solution.*

In addition, high-sociability communities often develop cliques and informal, behind-the-scenes networks that can circumvent or, worse, undermine due process in an organization. This is not to say that high-sociability companies lack formal organizational structures. Many of them are very hierarchical. But friendships and unofficial networks of friendships allow people to pull an end run around the hierarchy. For example, if a manager in sales hates the marketing department's new strategic plan, instead of explaining his or her opposition at a staff meeting, the manager might talk it over directly (over drinks, after work) to an old friend, the company's senior vice president. Suddenly the plan might be canceled without the marketing department's ever knowing why. In a best-case scenario, this kind of circumvention of systems lends a company a certain flexibility: maybe the marketing plan was lousy, and canceling it through official routes might have taken months. But in the worst case, it can be destructive to loyalty, commitment, and morale. In other words, networks can function well if you are an insider—you know the right people, hear the right gossip. Those on the outside often feel lost in the organization, mistreated by it, or simply unable to affect processes or products in any real way.

Solidarity, by contrast, is based not so much in the heart as in the mind, although it, too, can come naturally to groups in business settings. Its relationships are based on common tasks, mutual interests, or shared goals that will benefit all involved parties. Labor unions are a classic example of high-solidarity communities. Likewise, the solidarity of professionals—doctors and lawyers, for example—may be swiftly and ruthlessly mobilized if there is an outside competitive threat, such as proposed government regulations that could limit profitability. But, just as often, solidarity occurs between unlike individuals and groups and is not sustained by continuous social relations.

Consider the case of a Canadian clothing maker that wanted to identify strategies to expand internationally. Although its leaders were aware that the company's design, manufacturing, and marketing divisions had a long history of strained relations, they assigned two managers from each to a strategy SWAT team. Despite very little socializing and virtually no extraneous banter, the team worked fast and well together—and for good reason: each manager's bonus was based on the team's performance. After the group's report was done—its analysis and recommendations were top-notch—the managers returned to their jobs, never to associate again. In other words, solidarity can be demonstrated discontinuously, as the need arises. In contrast to sociability, then, it can be expressed both intermittently and contingently. It does not require daily display, nor does it necessarily rest upon a network of close friendships.

The organizational benefits of solidarity in a business community are many. Solidarity generates a high degree of strategic focus, swift response to competitive threats, and intolerance of poor performance. It also can result in a degree of ruthlessness. If the organization's strategy is correct, this kind of focused intent and action can be devastatingly effective. The ruthlessness, by the way, can itself reinforce solidarity: if everyone has to perform to strict standards, an equality-of-suffering effect may occur, building a sense of community in shared experience. Finally, when all employees are held to the same high standards, they often develop a strong sense of trust in the organization. This company treats everyone fairly and equally, the thinking goes; it is a meritocracy that cuts no special deals for favored or connected employees. In time, this trust can translate into commitment and loyalty to the organization's goals and purpose.

But, like sociability, solidarity has its costs as well. As we said above, strategic focus is good as long as it zeroes in on the right strategy. But if the strategy is not the right one, it is the equivalent of corporate suicide. Organizations can charge right over the cliff with great efficiency if they do the wrong things well. In addition, cooperation occurs in high-solidarity organizations only when the advantage to the individual is clear. Before taking on assignments or deciding how hard to work on projects, people ask, "What's in it for me?" If the answer is not obvious or immediate, neither is the response.

Finally, in high-solidarity organizations, roles (that is, job definitions) tend to be extremely clear. By contrast, in cultures where people are very friendly, roles and responsibilities tend to blur a bit. Someone in sales might become deeply involved in a new R&D project—a collaboration made possible by social ties. This kind of overlap usually doesn't happen in high-solidarity environments. Indeed, such environments are often characterized by turf battles, as individuals police and protect the boundaries of their roles. Someone in sales who tried to become involved in an R&D effort would be sent packing—and quickly.

One of the great errors of the recent literature on corporate culture has been to assume that organizations are homogeneous.

Although our discussion separates sociability and solidarity, many observers of organizational life confuse the two, and it is easy to see why. The concepts can, and often do, overlap. Social interaction at work may reflect the sociability of friends, the solidarity of colleagues, both, or—sometimes—neither. Equally, when colleagues socialize outside work, their interaction may represent an extension of workplace solidarity or an expression of intimate or close friendship. Yet to identify a community's culture correctly and to assess its appropriateness for the business environment, it is more than academic to assess sociability and solidarity as distinct measures. Asking the right questions can help in this process. (See the questionnaire "What Is Your Organization's Culture?")

It is critical, before completing the form, to select the parameters of the group you will be evaluating; for

---

What Is Your Organization's Culture?

To assess your organization's level of sociability, answer the following questions:	low	medium	high

1. People here try to make friends and to keep their relationships strong

2. People here get along very well

3. People in our group often socialize outside the office

4. People here really like one another

5. When people leave our group, we stay in touch

6. People here do favors for others because they like one another

7. People here often confide in one another about personal matters

To assess your organization's level of solidarity, answer the following questions:

1. Our group (organization, division, unit, team) understands and shares the same business objectives

2. Work gets done effectively and productively

3. Our group takes strong action to address poor performance

4. Our collective will to win is high

5. When opportunities for competitive advantage arise, we move quickly to capitalize on them

6. We share the same strategic goals

7. We know who the competition is

instance, you might assess your entire company with all its divisions and subgroups or a unit as small as a team. Either is fine, as long as you do not change horses in midstream. Our unit of analysis here is primarily the corporation, but we recognize that executives may use the framework to look inside their own organizations, comparing units, divisions, or other groups with one another.

Such an exercise can indeed be instructive. One of the great errors of the recent literature on corporate culture has been to assume that organizations are homogeneous. Just as one organization differs from another, so do units within them. For example, the R&D division of a pharmaceutical company might differ markedly from the manufacturing division in both solidarity and sociability. In addition, there are often hierarchical differences within a single company: senior managers may display an entirely different culture from middle managers, and different still from blue-collar workers.

Is this variation good news or bad news? The answer depends on the situation and requires managerial judgment. Radically different cultures inside a company may very well explain conflict and suggest that intervention is necessary. Similarly, one type of culture throughout a corporation may be a signal that some forms need to be adjusted to account for differing business environments.

The Networked Organization: High Sociability, Low Solidarity

It is perhaps the rituals of what we call networked organizations that are most noticeable to outsiders. People frequently stop to talk in the hallways; they wander into one another's offices with no purpose but to say hello;

lunch is an event in which groups often go out and dine together; and after-hours socializing is not the exception but the rule. Many of these organizations celebrate birthdays, field softball teams, and hold parties to honor an employee's long service or retirement. There may be nicknames, in-house jokes, or a common language drawn from shared experiences. (At one networked company, for instance, employees tease one another with the phrase "Don't pull a Richard," in reference to an employee who once fell asleep during a meeting. Richard himself uses the jest as well.) Employees in networked organizations sometimes act like family, attending one another's weddings, anniversary parties, and children's confirmations and bar mitzvahs. They may even live in the same towns. (See "Unilever: A Networked Organization," on page 34.)

Networked organizations are characterized not by a lack of hierarchy but by a profusion of ways to get around it.

Inside the office, networked cultures are characterized not by a lack of hierarchy but by a profusion of ways to get around it. Friends or cliques of friends make sure that decisions about issues are made before meetings are held to discuss them. People move from one position to another without the "required" training. Employees are hired without going through official channels in the human resources department—they know someone inside the network. As we have said, this informality can lend flexibility to an organization and be a healthy way of cutting through the bureaucracy. But it also means that the people in these cultures have developed two of the networked organization's key competencies: the ability to collect and selectively disseminate soft information, and the ability to acquire sponsors or allies in the company who will speak on their behalf both formally and informally.

What are the other hallmarks of networked organizations? Their low levels of solidarity mean that managers often have trouble getting functions or operating companies to cooperate. At one large European manufacturer, personal relations among senior executives of businesses in France, Italy, the United Kingdom, and Germany were extremely friendly. Several executives had known one another for years; some even took vacations together. But when the time came for corporate headquarters to parcel out resources, those same executives fought acrimoniously. At one point, they individually subverted attempts by headquarters to introduce a Europe-wide marketing strategy designed to combat the entry of U.S. competition.

Finally, a networked organization is usually so political that individuals and cliques spend much of their time pursuing personal agendas. It becomes hard for colleagues to agree on priorities and for managers to enforce them. It is not uncommon to hear frequent calls for strong leadership to overcome the divisions of subcultures, cliques, or warring factions in networked organizations.

In addition, because there is little commitment to shared business objectives, employees in networked organizations often contest performance measures, procedures, rules, and systems. For instance, at one international consumer-products company with which we have worked, the strategic planning process, the structural relationship between corporate headquarters and operating companies, and the accounting and budgetary control systems were heavily and continually criticized by executives in country businesses. Indeed, the criticism even took on an element of sport, increasing sociability among employees but doing nothing for the already diminished levels of solidarity.

Generally speaking, few organizations start their life cycle in the networked quadrant. By definition, sociability is built up over time. It follows, then, that many organizations migrate there from other quadrants. And despite the political nature of this kind of community, there are many examples of successful networked corporations. These organizations have learned how to overcome the negatives of sociability, such as cliques, gossip, and low productivity, and how to reap its benefits, such as increased creativity and commitment. One method of maximizing the benefits of a networked culture is to move individuals regularly between functions, businesses, and countries in order to limit excessive local identification and help them develop a wider strategic view of the organization. Later on, these individuals often become the primary managers of the networked organization's political processes, and they keep them healthy.

High levels of sociability usually go hand in hand with low solidarity because close friendships can inhibit the open expression of differences, the criticism of ideas, and forceful dissent. Constructive conflict, however, is often a precondition for developing and maintaining a shared sense of purpose—that is, solidarity. It would not be surprising, then, to find that well-meaning management interventions to increase strategic focus often consolidate workplace friendships but do little for organizational solidarity. That could account for at least some of the frustrations of those who complain, for example, that the outdoor team-building weekend was great fun but not remotely connected to the daily work of ensuring that the different parts of the business are integrated.

As we have noted, each type of corporate culture has its most appropriate time and place. We have observed that the networked organization functions well under the following business conditions:

- When corporate strategies have a long time frame. Sociability maintains allegiance to the organization when short-term calculations of interest do not. Consider the case of a company expanding into Vietnam. It might be years before such an effort is profitable, and in the meantime the process of getting operations running may be difficult and frustrating. In a networked culture, employees are often willing to put up with risk and discomfort. They are loyal to their colleagues in an open-ended way. The enjoyment of friendship on a daily basis is its own reward.

- When knowledge of the peculiarities of local markets is a critical success factor. The reason is that networked organizations are low on solidarity: members of one unit don't willingly share ideas or information with members of another. This would certainly be a strategic disadvantage if success came from employees having a broad, big-picture perspective. But when success is driven by deep and intense familiarity with a unit's home turf, low solidarity is no hindrance.

- When corporate success is an aggregate of local success. Again, this is a function of low solidarity. If headquarters can do well with low levels of interdivisional communication, then the networked culture is appropriate.

The Mercenary Organization: Low Sociability, High Solidarity

At the other end of the spectrum from the networked organization, the mercenary community is low on hallway hobnobbing and high on data-laden memos. Indeed, almost all communication in a mercenary organization is focused on business matters. The reason: individual interests coincide with corporate objectives, and those objectives are often linked to a crystal clear perception of the "enemy" and the steps required to beat it. As a result, mercenary organizations are characterized by the ability to respond quickly and cohesively to a perceived opportunity or threat in the marketplace. Priorities are decided swiftly—generally by senior management—and enforced throughout the organization with little debate.

In mercenary organizations, you rarely hear, for instance, "It was a shame we had to let John go—he was so nice."

Mercenary organizations are also characterized by a clear separation of work and social life. (Interestingly, these cultures often consist of people whose work takes priority over their private life.) Members of this kind of business community rarely fraternize outside the office, and if they do, it is at functions organized around business, such as a party to celebrate the defeat of a competitor or the successful implementation of a strategic plan. (See "Mastiff Wear: A Mercenary Organization," on page 38.)

Because of the absence of strong personal ties, mercenary organizations are generally intolerant of poor performance. Those who are not contributing fully are fired or given explicit instructions on how to improve, with a firm deadline. There is a hard-heartedness to this aspect of mercenary cultures, and yet the high levels of commitment to a common purpose mean it is accepted, and usually supported, in the ranks. If someone has not performed, you rarely hear, for instance, "It was a shame we had to let John go—he was so nice." John, the thinking would be, wasn't doing his part toward clearly stated, shared strategic objectives.

Finally, the low level of social ties means that mercenary organizations are rarely bastions of loyalty. Employees may very well respect and like their organizations; after all, these institutions are usually fair to those who work hard and meet standards. But those feelings are not sentimental or tied to affectionate relationships between individuals. People stay with high-solidarity companies for as long as their personal needs are met, and then they move on.

Without a doubt, the advantages of a mercenary organization can sound seductive in the performance-driven 1990s. What manager would not want his or her company to have a heightened sense of competition and a strong will to win? In addition, because of their focused activity, many mercenary organizations are very productive. Moreover, unhindered by friendships, employees are not reluctant to compete, further enhancing performance as standards get pushed ever higher.

But mercenary communities have disadvantages as well. Employees who are busy chasing specific targets are often disinclined to cooperate, share information, or exchange new or creative ideas. To do so would be a distraction. Cooperation between units with different goals is even less likely. Consider the example of Warner Brothers, the entertainment conglomerate. The music and film divisions, each with its own strategic targets, have trouble achieving synergy—for example, with sound tracks. (Musicians recording on a Warner record label, for instance, might be called on to score a Warner movie.) Compare this situation with that at Disney, a major competitor, which relentlessly and profitably exploits synergies between its movie characters—from Snow White to Simba—and its merchandising divisions.

The mercenary organization works effectively under the following business conditions:

- When change is fast and rampant. This type of situation calls for a rapid, focused response, which a mercenary organization is able to mount.

- When economies of scale are achieved, or competitive advantage is gained, through creating corporate centers of excellence that can impose processes and procedures on operating companies or divisions. For example, the Zürich-based diversified corporation ABB Asea Brown Boveri builds worldwide centers of excellence for product groups. Its Finnish subsidiary Stromberg has become the world leader in electric drives since its acquisition in 1986, and it now sets the standard for the ABB empire.

- When corporate goals are clear and measurable, and there is therefore little need for input from the ranks or for consensus building.

- When the nature of the competition is clear. Mercenary organizations thrive when the enemy—and the best way to defeat it—are obvious. The mercenary organization is most appropriate when one enemy can be distinguished from many. Komatsu, for example, made *Maru-C*—translated as "Encircle Caterpillar"—its war cry back in 1965 and focused all its strategic efforts during the 1970s and early 1980s on doing just that, aided effectively by a high-solidarity culture. By contrast, IBM zigzagged strategically for years, unable to identify its competition until the game was nearly up. Its cultural type during that time is not known to us, but we can guess with confidence that it wasn't mercenary.

The Fragmented Organization: Low Sociability, Low Solidarity

Few managers would volunteer to work for or, perhaps harder still, run a fragmented organization. But like strife-ridden countries, unfriendly neighborhoods, and disharmonious families, such communities are a fact of life. What are their primary characteristics in a business setting?

Perhaps most notably, employees of fragmented organizations display a low consciousness of organizational membership. They often believe that they work for themselves or they identify with occupational groups— usually professional.

People in fragmented organizations often work with their doors shut or at home.

Asked at a party what he does for a living, for instance, a doctor at a major teaching hospital that happens to have this kind of culture might reply, "I'm a surgeon," leaving out the name of the institution where he is employed. Likewise, organizations that have this kind of culture rarely field softball teams—who would want to wear the company's name on a T-shirt?—and employees engage in none of the extracurricular rites and rituals that characterize high-sociability cultures, considering them a waste of time. (See "University Business School: A Fragmented Organization," on page 40.)

This lack of affective interrelatedness extends to behavior on the job. People work with their doors shut or, in many cases, at home, going to the office only to collect mail or make long-distance calls. They are often secretive about their projects and progress with coworkers, offering information only when asked point-blank. In extreme cases, members of fragmented organizations have such low levels of sociability that they attempt to sabotage the work of their "colleagues" through gossip, rumor, or overt criticism delivered to higher-ups in the organization.

This culture also has low levels of solidarity: its members rarely agree about organizational objectives, critical success factors, and performance standards. It's no surprise, then, that high levels of dissent about strategic goals often make these organizations difficult to manage top-down. Leaders often feel isolated and routinely report feeling as if there is no action they can take to effect change. Their calls fall on deaf ears.

Low sociability also means that individuals may give of themselves on a personal level only after careful calculation of what they might get in return. Retirement parties, for example, are often sparsely attended. Indeed, any social behavior that is discretionary is unlikely to take place.

We realize it must sound as if fragmented organizations are wretched places to work—or at least appeal only to the hermits or Scrooges of the business world. But situations do exist that invite, or even benefit from, such a culture, and further, this kind of environment is attractive to individuals who prefer to work alone or to keep their work and personal lives entirely separate.

In our research, we have seen fragmented organizations operate successfully in several forms. First, the culture functions well in manufacturing concerns that rely heavily on the outsourcing of piecework. Second, the culture can succeed in professional organizations, such as consulting and law firms, in which highly trained individuals have idiosyncratic work styles. Third, fragmented cultures often accompany organizations that have become virtual: employees work either at home or on the road, reporting in to a central base mainly by electronic means. Of course, fragmented organizations sometimes reflect dysfunctional communities in which ties of sociability or solidarity have been torn asunder by organizational politics, downsizing, or other forms of disruption. In these cases, the old ties of friendship and loyalty are replaced by an overriding concern for individual survival, unleashing a war of all against all.

The last unhealthy scenario aside, however, a fragmented culture is appropriate under the following business conditions:

- When there is little interdependence in the work itself. This might occur, for example, in a company in which pieces of furniture or clothing are subcontracted to individuals who work out of their homes and then assembled at another site. A second example might be a firm composed of tax lawyers, each working for different clients.

- When significant innovation is produced primarily by individuals rather than by teams. (This, it should be noted, is becoming increasingly rare in business, as cross-disciplinary teams demonstrate the power of *unlike* minds working together.)

- When standards are achieved by input controls, not process controls. In these organizations, time has proven that management's focus should be on recruiting the right people; once they have been hired and trained, their work requires little supervision. They are their own best judges, their own harshest taskmasters.

- When there are few learning opportunities between individuals or when professional pride prevents the transfer of knowledge. In an international oil-trading company we have worked with, for example, employees who traded Nigerian oil never shared market information with employees trading Saudi crude. For one thing, they weren't given any incentive to take the time to do so; for another, each group of traders took pride in knowing more than the other. To give away information was to give away the prestige of being at the top of the field—a market insider.

The Communal Organization: High Sociability, High Solidarity

A communal culture can evolve at any stage of a company's life cycle, but when we are asked to illustrate this form, we often cite the characteristics of a typical small, fast-growing, entrepreneurial start-up. The founders and early employees of such companies are close friends, working endless hours in tight quarters. This kinship usually flows into close ties outside the office. In the early days of Apple Computer, for instance, employees lived together, commuted together, and spent weekends together, too. At the same time, the sense of solidarity at a typical start-up is sky high. A tiny company has one or at most two products and just as few goals (the first usually being survival). Because founders and early employees often have equity in the start-up, success has clear, collective benefits. In communal organizations, everything feels in sync.

But, as we have said, start-ups don't own this culture. Indeed, communal cultures can be found in mature companies in which employees have worked together for decades to develop both friendships and mutually beneficial objectives. (See "British-Borneo Petroleum Syndicate: A Communal Organization," on page 42.)

Regardless of their stage of development, communal organizations share certain traits. First, their employees possess a high, sometimes exaggerated, consciousness of organizational identity and membership. Individuals may even link their sense of self with the corporate identity. Some employees at Nike, it is said, have the company's trademark symbol tattooed above their ankles. Similarly, in the early days of Apple Computer, employees readily identified themselves as "Apple people."

Organizational life in communal companies is punctuated by social events that take on a strong ritual significance. The London office of the international advertising agency J. Walter Thompson, for instance, throws parties for its staff at exciting, even glamorous, locations; recent events were held at the Hurlingham Club and the Natural History Museum in London. The company also offers its employees a master class on creativity that features a speech by a celebrity. Dave Stewart, former guitarist of the rock band the Eurythmics, even played a set during his presentation. And finally, Thompson holds an annual gala awards ceremony for the company's best creative teams. Winners go to lunch in Paris. Other communal companies celebrate entrance into their organizations and promotions with similar fanfare.

The high solidarity of communal cultures is often demonstrated through an equitable sharing of risks and rewards among employees. Communal organizations, after all, place an extremely high value on fairness and justice, which comes into sharp focus particularly in hard times. For example, during the 1970 recession, rather than lay people off, Hewlett-Packard introduced a 10% cut in pay and hours across every rank. It should be noted that the company's management did not become demonized or despised in the process. In fact, what happened at Hewlett-Packard is another characteristic of communal companies: their leaders command widespread respect, deference, and even affection. Although they invite dissent, and even succeed in receiving it, their authority is rarely challenged.

Solidarity also shows itself clearly when it comes to company goals and values. The mission statement is often given front-and-center display in a communal company's offices, and it evokes enthusiasm rather than cynicism.

Finally, in communal organizations, employees are very clear about the competition. They know which companies threaten theirs—what they do well, how they are weak—and how they can be overcome. And not only is the external competition seen clearly, its defeat is also perceived to be a matter of competing values. The competition has as much to do with an organization's purpose—the reason it exists—as it has with winning market share or increasing operating margins.

Given all these characteristics, it is perhaps not surprising that many managers see the communal organization as the ideal. Solidarity alone may be symptomatic of excessive instrumentalism. Employees may withdraw their cooperation the moment they become unable to identify shared advantage. In some cases, particularly where there are well-established performance-related reward systems, this attitude may be reflected in an exaggerated concern with those activities that produce measurable outcomes. By contrast, organizations that are characterized primarily by sociability may lose their sense of purpose.

There may be a built-in tension between sociability and solidarity that makes communal cultures inherently unstable.

However, where both sociability and solidarity are high, a company gets the best of both worlds—or does it? The answer is that the communal culture may be an inappropriate and unattainable ideal in many business contexts. Our research suggests that it seems to work best in religious, political, and civic organizations. It is much harder to find commercial enterprises in this quadrant. The reason is that many businesses that achieve the communal form find it difficult to sustain. There are a number of possible explanations. First, high levels of sociability and solidarity are often formed around particular founders or leaders whose departure may weaken either or both forms of social relationship. Second, the high-sociability half of the communal culture is often antithetical to what goes on inside an organization during periods of growth, diversification, or internationalization. These massive and complex change efforts require focus, urgency, and performance—the stuff of solidarity in its undiluted form.

More profoundly, though, there may be a built-in tension between relationships of sociability and solidarity that makes the communal business enterprise an inherently unstable form. The sincere geniality of sociability doesn't usually coexist—it can't—with solidarity's dispassionate, sometimes ruthless focus on achievement of goals. When the two do coexist, as we have said, it is often in religious or volunteer groups. Perhaps one reason is that people tend to join these groups after they've become familiar with, and agree with, their objectives. (A church's policies, procedures, beliefs, and goals, for instance, are made well known to prospective members before they join. Once inside the organization, members find little "strategic" dissension to get in the way of friendship.) By contrast, when people consider employment at a business enterprise, they may not know what the organization's beliefs and values are—or they may know them and disagree with them but join the organization anyway for financial or career reasons. Over time, their objections may manifest themselves in low-solidarity behaviors.

In their attempts to mimic the virtues of communal organizations, many senior managers have failed to think through whether high levels of both sociability and solidarity are, in fact, what they need. Again, from our research, it is clear that the desirable mix varies according to the context. In what situations, then, does a communal culture function well?

- When innovation requires elaborate and extensive teamwork across functions and perhaps locations. Increasingly, high-impact innovation cannot be achieved by isolated specialists. Rather, as the knowledge base of organizations deepens and diversifies, many talents need to combine (and combust) for truly creative change. For example, at the pharmaceutical company Glaxo Wellcome, research projects are undertaken by teams from different disciplines—such as genetics, chemistry, and toxicology—and in different locations. Without such teamwork, drug development would be much slower and competitive advantage would be lost.

- When there are real synergies among organizational subunits and real opportunities for learning. We emphasize the word *real* because synergy and learning are often held up as organizational goals without hard scrutiny. Both are good—in theory. In practice, opportunities for synergy and learning among one company's divisions may not actually exist or be worth the effort. However, when they do exist, a communal culture unquestionably helps.

- When strategies are more long-term than short-term. That is to say, when corporate goals won't be reached in the foreseeable future, managerial mechanisms are needed to keep commitment and focus high. The communal culture provides high sociability to bolster relationships (and the commitment that accompanies them) and high solidarity to sustain focus. Indeed, we have seen communal cultures help enormously as organizations have gone global—a long and often tortuous process during which strategies have a tendency to be open ended and emergent, as opposed to the sum of measurable milestones.

- When the business environment is dynamic and complex. Although many organizations claim to be in such an environment, it is perhaps most pronounced in sectors like information technology, telecommunications, and pharmaceuticals. In these industries, organizations interface with their environment through multiple connections involving technology, customers, the government, competition, and research institutes. A communal culture is appropriate in this kind of environment because its dynamics aid in the synthesis of information from all these sources.

Changing the Culture

There is clearly an implied argument here that organizations should strive for a form of community suited to their environment. Reality is never so neat. In fact, managers continually face the challenge of adjusting their corporate community to a changing environment. Our research suggests that over the last decade, a number of large, well-established companies with strong traditions of loyalty and collegiality have been forced, mostly through competitive threat, to move from the networked to the mercenary form. To describe the process as tricky does not do it justice. It is perhaps one of the most complex and risk-laden changes a manager can face.

Consider the example of chairman and president Jan D. Timmer of the Dutch electronics company Philips. Once a monumentally successful company, Philips lost its competitive edge in the mid-1980s and even came close to collapse. Timmer (and many observers) attributed much of the company's troubles to its corporate culture. Sociability was so extreme that highly politicized cliques ruled and healthy information flow stopped, particularly between R&D and marketing. (During this period, many of Philips's new products flopped; critics said the reason was that they provided technology that consumers didn't particularly want.) Meanwhile, authority was routinely challenged, as were company goals and strategies. Management's lack of control allowed many employees to relax on the job. They had little concern with performance standards and no sense of competitive threat. In short, Philips demonstrated many of the negative consequences of a networked organization. However, given the industry's primary success factors—innovation, market focus, and fast product rollout—Philips needed a mercenary or communal culture to stay even, not to mention get ahead.

Timmer attempted just such a transformation, first by trying to lower managers' comfort level. He implemented measurable, ambitious performance targets and held individuals accountable to them. In the process, many long-serving executives left the company or were sidelined. Timmer also conducted frequent management conferences, at which the company's objectives, procedures, and values were clearly communicated. He demanded commitment to these goals, and those employees who did not conform were let go. In this way, solidarity was increased, and Philips's performance began to show it.

As performance began to improve markedly, Timmer made efforts to restore some of the company's sociability, which had been lost during the turnaround—thus moving the company from mercenary toward communal. Meetings began to focus on the company's values and on gaining consensus. In short, Timmer was try-

> *How does an organization change its culture from one type to another without wreaking too much damage?*

ing to reestablish loyalty to Philips and connections among its members. Timmer was scheduled to retire in October, and it remains to be seen in what direction his successor, Cor Boonstra, will take the company.

Boonstra's challenge is formidable. Once organizations try to reduce well-established ties of sociability, they can inadvertently unleash a process that is difficult to control. Unpicking emotional relationships may make solidarity difficult, too. The result: organizations can devolve toward an inappropriate fragmented form. From there, recovery can be difficult.

This precise phenomenon, in fact, can be seen in the uncomfortable transition now occurring in the British Broadcasting Corporation. Its director general, John Birt, has tried to focus the organization—long known for its quality programming and public service—on efficiency and productivity. In the process, strict performance standards have been set, and colleagues have had to vie against one another for scarcer resources. As sociability has diminished, talented individuals who once saw themselves as part of a communal culture have railed against what they consider target-oriented changes. Some have decided to stay and stubbornly defend their own interests; others have chosen to leave. With its communal culture heading toward a fragmented one, the BBC faces no alternative but to reinvent itself.

How, then, does an organization change its culture from one type to another without wreaking too much damage? How does a manager tweak levels of sociability or solidarity?

Clearly, the tools required to manipulate each dimension are different. And using them involves understanding why a culture has taken its current form in the first place—why, that is, a culture possesses its present levels of sociability and solidarity. Neighborhoods, book clubs, and *Fortune* 100 companies can all be friendly for myriad reasons—the example set by a leader, the personalities of certain members, the physical setting of the organization or its history, or simply the amount of cash in the bank. Likewise, solidarity can arise for many reasons. Our purpose here has been not to analyze *why* organizations have different levels of sociability and solidarity but to examine *what happens* to their culture when they do, and what that means for managers who seek satisfied employees and strong performance. However, before attempting to change levels of sociability or solidarity, a manager needs to think a bit like a doctor taking on a new patient. The patient's past and current conditions are not only relevant but also critically important to assessing the best future treatment.

Our research shows that to increase sociability, managers can take the following steps:

Promote the sharing of ideas, interests, and emotions by recruiting compatible people—people who naturally seem likely to become friends. Before hiring a candidate, for instance, a manager might arrange for him or her to have lunch with several current employees in order to get a sense of the chemistry among them. This kind of activity need not be covert. Trying to find employees who share interests and attitudes can even be stated as an explicit goal. In itself, such an announcement may signal that management seeks to increase sociability.

Increase social interaction among employees by arranging casual gatherings inside and outside the office, such as parties, excursions—even book clubs. These events might be awkward at first, as employees question their purpose or simply feel odd associating outside a business setting. One way around this problem is to schedule such gatherings during work hours so that attendance is essentially mandatory. It is also critical to make these interactions enjoyable so that they create their own positive, self-reinforcing dynamic. The hard news for managers is that sometimes this orchestrated socializing requires spending money, which can be difficult to rationalize to the finance department. However, if the business environment demands higher levels of sociability, managers can consider the expenditure a good investment in long-term profitability.

Reduce formality between employees. Managers can encourage informal dress codes, arrange offices differently, or designate spaces where employees can mingle on equal terms, such as the lunchroom or gym.

Limit hierarchical differences. There are several means to this end. For one, the organization chart can be redesigned to eliminate layers and ranks. Also, hierarchy has a hard time coexisting with shared facilities and open office layouts. Some companies have narrowed hierarchical differences by ensuring that all employees, regardless of rank, receive the same package of benefits, park in the same lot (with no assigned spaces), and get bonuses based on the same formula.

Act like a friend yourself, and set the example for geniality and kindness by caring for those in trouble. At one communal company we know of, management gave a three-month paid leave of absence to an employee whose young son was ill, and then allowed her to work on a flexible schedule until he was completely well. Sociability is increased when this caring extends beyond crisis situations—for instance, when management welcomes the families of its employees into the fold by inviting them to company picnics or outings. Indeed, many high-sociability companies hold Christmas parties for the children of employees or give each family a special holiday present.

To build solidarity, managers can take the following steps:

Develop awareness of competitors through briefings, newsletters, videos, memos, or E-mail. For example, as Timmer worked to move Philips toward the mercenary form, he exhorted his managers to take a new, hard look at the company's Japanese competitors. Breaking a longtime organizational taboo, he praised Japanese quality highly and compared Japanese products favorably with those his company made.

Create a sense of urgency. Managers can promote a sense of urgency in their people by developing a visionary statement or slogan for the organization and communicating it relentlessly. In the late 1980s, for example, Gerard van Schaik, then chairman of the board of Heineken, took his company global with the internal war cry Paint the World Green. The message was clear, focused, and action oriented. It worked. Today Heineken is the most international beer company in the world.

Stimulate the will to win. Managers can hire and promote individuals with drive or ambition, set high standards for performance, and celebrate success in high-profile ways. Mary Kay, the Texas-based cosmetics company, is famous for giving its top saleswomen pink Cadillacs. In most other organizations, a large check or public recognition—or both—does the same job. Similarly, an incentive system that rewards corporate performance (rather than or in addition to unit and personal performance) underscores the importance of the company's overall achievement.

Encourage commitment to shared corporate goals.
To do so, managers can move people between functions, businesses, and countries to reduce strong subcultures and create a sense of one company. Disney, for example, identifies highfliers—candidates that show promise— and then moves them through five divisions in five years. These individuals then carry the organization's larger strategic picture and purpose with them throughout their later positions at Disney, pollinating each division in the process.

Building the Right Community

So far, we have stressed three primary points. First, knowing how your organization measures up on the dimensions of sociability and solidarity is an important managerial competence. Second, knowing whether the company's culture fits the business environment is critical to competitive advantage. And third, there is no golden quadrant that guarantees success. We must stress, however, that our model for analyzing culture and its fit with the business context is a dynamic one. Business environments do not stay the same. Similarly, organizations have life cycles. Successful organizations need a sense not just of where they are but of where they are heading. This demands a subtle appreciation of human relations and an awareness that manipulating sociability on the one hand and solidarity on the other involves very different challenges.

Finally, we have claimed that patterns of organizational life are often conditioned by factors outside the organization, such as the competition, the industry structure, and the pace of technological change. But a company's culture is also governed by choices. Senior executives cannot avoid or deny this fact. Managers can increase the amount of sociability in their staffs by employing many of the devices listed above; similarly, they can manipulate levels of solidarity through the decisions they make. In short, these choices have the ability to affect what kinds of experiences members of an organization enjoy—and don't—on a day-to-day basis. Executives are therefore left with the job of managing the tension between creating a culture that produces a winning organization and creating one that makes people happy and allows the authentic expression of individual values. This challenge is profound and personal, and its potential for impact on performance is enormous. Culture *can* hold back the pressures for corporate disintegration if managers understand what culture means—and what it means to change it.

Unilever: A Networked Organization

THERE IS A FREQUENTLY TOLD STORY WITHIN UNILEVER, the Anglo-Dutch consumer-goods group with worldwide sales of roughly $50 billion. Unilever executives, it is said, recognize one another at airports, even when they've never met before. There's something about the way they look and act—something so subtle it's impossible to pin down in words yet unmistakable to those who have worked for the company for more than a few years.

Obviously, there's a bit of exaggeration in this company legend, but it underscores Unilever's tradition as a networked company—that is, one with a culture characterized by high levels of sociability. For years, the company has explicitly recruited compatible people—people with similar backgrounds, values, and interests. Unilever's managers believe that this corps of like-minded individuals is the reason why its employees work so well together despite their national diversity, why they demonstrate such strong loyalty to their colleagues, and why they embrace the company's values of cooperation and consensus.

Unilever takes other steps to reinforce and increase the sociability in its ranks. At Four Acres, the company's international-management-training center outside London, hundreds of executives a year partake in activities rich in social rituals: multicourse dinners, group photographs, sports on the lawn, and, perhaps above all, a bar that literally never closes. As former chairman Floris Maljers remarks, "This shared experience creates an informal network of equals who know one another well and usually continue to meet and exchange experiences."

In addition to the events at Four Acres, Unilever's sociability is bolstered by annual conferences attended by the company's top 500 managers. The company's leaders use these meetings to communicate and review strategy, but there is much more to them than work. (The intense fraternizing that takes place at these conferences has earned them the nickname Oh! Be Joyfuls!) Maljers notes, "Over good food and drink, our most senior people meet, exchange views, and reconfirm old friendships."

Finally, Unilever moves its young managers frequently —across borders, products, and divisions. This effort is an attempt to start Unilever relationships early, as well as to increase know-how.

Yet these carefully nurtured patterns of sociability have not always been matched by high levels of company-wide solidarity. Unilever has found it hard over the years to achieve cross-company coordination and agreement on objectives. It's not that executives fight over strategy as much as "talk it to death" in the search for consensus, says one senior vice president.

Does this networked culture fit Unilever's business environment? In good part, yes. Unilever's managers hail from dozens of countries. This diversity could have been an isolating factor, hindering the flow of information and ideas. But because of the culture's high levels of sociability, there is widespread fellowship and goodwill instead. Second, a key success factor in Unilever's business is proximity to local markets. The organization's low solidarity has kept units focused on their home bases with good results. And finally, until recently, Unilever has been a highly decentralized organization. Simply put, there has been little need for strategic agreement among units.

But Unilever's environment might very well be changing with the emergence of a single European market, which would make coordination among businesses and functions imperative. Indeed, many recent organizational changes—the creation of Lever Europe in the detergents business, for example—can be interpreted as an attempt by Unilever to create higher levels of corporate solidarity, largely through a process of centralization.

In addition, Unilever faces some competitors, such as Procter & Gamble and L'Oréal, known for their high levels of solidarity around corporate goals. This asset has lent Unilever's competitors the ability to accelerate product development processes and exploit market opportunities quickly. Unilever must match those competencies or risk losing clout.

Finally, Unilever's relative lack of solidarity means that management can lose its sense of urgency—a competitive advantage in any business environment. This challenge is well known to the company's leaders. As

Maljers himself notes, "Everybody may be so busy with friends elsewhere—with the interesting training program, the well-organized course, the next major conference—that complacency sets in. Unfortunately, we have seen this happen in some of our units, especially the more successful ones. It may be necessary to shake up the system from time to time."

This comment underlines one of the biggest risks of the networked organization. Employees may be so busy being friends that they lose sight of the reason they are at work in the first place.

Interestingly, Unilever's recently announced organizational restructuring is designed in part to address some of the negative consequences of the networked form. The company will be broken into 14 business groups, and, according to the plan, each will have a clear business rationale, stretch targets, and transparent accountability. In a booklet sent to all managers, the company described the changes as a means to "establish a simple, effective organization dedicated to the needs of the future. This must provide great clarity of roles, responsibilities, and decision making. . . . Under the new structure, business groups will make annual contracts on which they must deliver come 'hell or high water.'"

Similarly, in an interview in the September issue of *Unilever* magazine, company chairman Niall FitzGerald identified the values of the new organization in these words: "Simplicity, clarity, and delegation of authority are intended to be the prime virtues of the new organization. A disciplined approach [is essential]—those who have been given the task of delivering results must focus on delivering."

In the terms of our model, this reorganization is clearly an effort to move toward the mercenary quadrant: less politicking (as enjoyable as it might be) and a more ruthless focus on results. But can Unilever let go of its ingrained sociability and take on the behaviors of a high-solidarity enterprise? The company's future performance will tell.

***

Mastiff Wear: A Mercenary Organization

SEVERAL YEARS AGO, A SENIOR MANAGER at a company we'll call Mastiff Wear, an international manufacturer of popular children's clothing, invited 15 of the company's top executives to dinner at a fancy new restaurant in London. The men and women had just sat down when the host announced a challenge to be completed over dinner: devise a new advertising slogan. The best solution, the host said, would earn a bottle of Dom Pérignon. For the next three hours, the guests took to their task single-mindedly, even tearing up the elegant menus to use as working paper. The restaurant's delicacies passed before them throughout the night, and the executives ate, but few seemed to take notice of where they were. What they were doing was all that mattered.

Not long after, one of the authors of this article met with a similar group of executives at Mastiff Wear. "If I join Mastiff next Monday," he asked them, "what should I know are the rules of success at this organization?" Rule one, he was told: Arrive on Sunday. Rule two: Call your family and tell them you won't be home until next weekend.

Both of these stories illustrate a typical mercenary culture in action: members work long hours and often value work over family life. (The executives in the restaurant worked even when they could have been socializing, and no one complained—or even noticed.) In addition, the stories illustrate this form's high degree of internal competition and strong focus on the achievement of tasks.

Mastiff also embodies several other characteristics of high-solidarity cultures. There are strict standards for performance, and underachievers are dealt with ruthlessly. As one executive remarks, "Once in a while, one of us just disappears." Those who survive are well rewarded—so well that many are able to retire early. Indeed, a common strategy for a Mastiff executive is to work hard, even at the cost of his or her personal life, accumulate wealth, and then leave. Relationships with the organization exist primarily as a means for employees to promote their own interests—career, personal, or otherwise.

In some ways, this mercenary culture has been an apt fit for Mastiff in recent years. The company has had considerable success in the clearly defined distribution channels in which it operates. Internally, a fierce focus on efficiency has ensured that resources are used to the fullest. Little is wasted, and the company does only what it can do best, creating centers of corporate excellence to spread its knowledge. Externally, a strategy of targeting clearly defined sectors—primarily department stores and catalogs—and a clearly identified "enemy" has consistently enabled Mastiff to establish dominant market positions. Most recently, this ability has been illustrated by the company's dramatic entry into the European market—a move that has inflicted considerable damage on a major competitive player there.

But mercenary cultures have their shortcomings. When you successfully occupy the number one position in many markets, as Mastiff has for many years, you may run out of enemies. As a result, you may lose the competitive edge that originally brought your company a sense of urgency and the collective will to win. In addition, Mastiff, like many mercenary cultures, may have suffered from excessive strategic focus. In this case, a characteristic concern with operational efficiencies proved barely adequate when competitors were gaining market share from new-product development. Focusing on one or two issues is a strength, of course. The danger is that you can lose sight of what's happening on the horizon.

University Business School: A Fragmented Organization

DESPITE HOW UNPLEASANT IT SOUNDS to work where both sociability and solidarity are lacking, there are indeed environments that invite such cultures and do no harm whatsoever to the organization, its people, or its products in the process. Still, there is the stigma of an "unfriendly" organization to contend with, which is the reason this case study uses a disguised name for its subject.

University Business School is typical of its breed: it offers an M.B.A. program and several shorter executive programs. Its other products are books, reports, and scholarly articles. The school achieves all this smoothly, with remarkably low levels of social interaction of any kind among members of the community.

Take sociability. At UBS, professors work mainly on their own, researching their specialty, preparing classes, writing articles, and assessing students' papers. Often this work is done at home or in the office, behind closed doors displaying Do Not Disturb signs. Many professors have demanding second jobs as consultants to industry. Therefore, when social contact does occur, it is with clients, students, or research sponsors rather than with colleagues. In fact, faculty members may actively avoid sociability on campus in order to maximize discretionary time for private consulting work and research for publication.

As for solidarity, UBS professors see themselves foremost as part of an international group of scholars, feeling no particular affinity for the institution that employs them. Their occupational group, they believe, sets the standards and controls outputs, such as journal articles. In addition, it shapes employment opportunities and determines career progress. There is no point, the professors' thinking goes, concerning themselves with the goals and strategies of an institution that does not have direct bearing on their day-to-day work or future pursuits.

As we have said, however, none of this diminished sociability or solidarity compromises the competitive position of UBS, a highly renowned institution. The reason is that many professors do indeed do their best work alone or with scholars from other institutions who share similar interests. Moreover, M.B.A. and other academic programs don't necessarily need input from groups of staff members; most professors know what to teach and are disinclined in any case to take the advice of others. Indeed, the only reason for meetings in this environment is to decide on academic appointments and promotions. This activity involves consideration of scholarship, which requires neither sociability nor solidarity. Finally, UBS need not worry that its employees are losing focus or urgency about their work—one of the biggest risks of low-solidarity organizations. On the contrary. UBS attracts a self-selecting group of highly autonomous, sometimes ego-centric individuals who are motivated, not alienated, by the freedoms of the fragmented organization.

In short, the success of UBS underscores our point: there is no generic ideal when it comes to corporate community. If the culture fits, wear it.

British-Borneo Petroleum Syndicate: A Communal Organization

SYNERGY IS A TERM THAT GETS BANDIED about quite a bit, as in "Wouldn't it be terrific if our divisions, operating companies, or functional areas had more synergy? Then they could learn from one another and share new ideas—even exchange market or technological information." This hope, while admirable in theory, often remains just that in practice—a hope.

Not so at British-Borneo Petroleum Syndicate, where a communal culture—combining high sociability and high solidarity—dovetails effectively with the company's strategic need for cooperation and interchange among functions and locations. Indeed, the synergy among groups at British-Borneo is perhaps its greatest competitive advantage. The London-based company, which has grown more than tenfold in the 1990s to reach a market capitalization of $550 million in 1996, explores for and produces oil and gas in the North Sea and the Gulf of Mexico. Success in this kind of endeavor arises from speed of movement, risk management, and the innovative use of technology—which in this context can come only out of cross-functional teams. Success is also linked to well-orchestrated, complex interfaces with other players in the market and with governments. And finally, success comes from employees committing to strategies that are rather long-term. The exploration phase for most ventures will take several years, and production—hence cash flow—often lags a few years beyond that.

British-Borneo's high levels of sociability can be seen in the honest and relaxed way employees interact. They talk about their feelings openly and often help one another out—without making deals. In addition, they are a team that plays together out of the office—at picnics, parties, and ball games. This conviviality is, in some part, management's doing. Managers have systematically tried to recruit compatible people with similar interests and backgrounds. And they have improved on this foundation with regular team-building events such as Outward Bound courses for all new hires, frequent social events, and active support of company softball, track, and sailing teams. Everyone in the company is invited to participate, from board members to clerks.

British-Borneo's sociability, however, has not come at the expense of solidarity. The company's employees display a strong sense of urgency and will to win. They are clearly committed to a common purpose. Indeed, in the United Kingdom, the company's strategy is known and understood by people of every rank, including secretaries and other support personnel. The widespread knowledge and acceptance of British-Borneo's objectives have come about through careful effort. The company devotes considerable time and energy to hammering out—through workshops and brainstorming sessions—a collective vision that is owned by the staff.

Interestingly, despite the company's high levels of sociability, British-Borneo employees are not reluctant to speak their mind. (Ordinarily, friendships preclude tough criticism or disagreement.) Staff members are encouraged to strip things down to reality when they communicate about the company's business. This frankness creates an atmosphere of challenge and debate, which is one of the hallmarks of a high-solidarity environment.

Finally, British-Borneo is a classic high-solidarity environment in its adherence to strict performance standards. The culture does not tolerate underachievement. Outstanding results are generously rewarded, but it is not unusual for someone who does not measure up to be asked to leave, sooner rather than later.

We've mentioned some of the sources of British-Borneo's culture, but it is critical to note that perhaps the most important source is CEO Alan Gaynor, whose charismatic leadership sets an example. Gaynor participates in the company's many social functions, for example, and is open about his feelings. At the same time, he is intolerant of subpar performance and is relentlessly focused on strategic goals.

That Gaynor is a major driver of British-Borneo's communal culture, however, is emblematic of one of this form's challenges. While a communal culture is usually difficult to attain and sustain, a strong leader can manage both to powerfully effective ends. But should the leader ever leave, the community he or she created can easily collapse. Because of its fragility, a communal culture is also difficult to export. That is the challenge Gaynor faces today, in fact, as British-Borneo's embryonic operations in Houston, Texas, go through a dramatic expansion.

Originally published in November–December 1996
Reprint 96605

Pygmalion in Management

J. STERLING LIVINGSTON

Executive Summary

EACH YEAR HBR PICKS AN ARTICLE from its repertoire of articles at least 15 years old and reprints it as a "Classic." In the 24 years that the magazine has been carrying out this practice, the articles selected have met these criteria: enduring value, wide application of and interest in the problem or issue considered, large number of reprints sold (indicating lasting acceptance), and frequent printed reference in books and other publications.

This year we present a remarkable analysis dating from the July–August 1969 issue. Its reprint history attests to its continued worth; orders for reprints still pour in, and to date HBR has distributed more than three-quarters of a million copies from some 9,500 orders.

The reprints are often found in the list of readings in executive development programs. And there's no surprise in that: Livingston focuses on the power of managers' expectations in training, teaching, and encouraging subordinates to improve themselves and preparing them for more responsible and more rewarding positions. There are skills to be learned that have been shown to succeed in getting lower-level managers and the rank-and-file to achieve superior performance and enhance their careers.

There are no secrets to success here, Livingston shows; enthusiasm and interest on the boss's part are the main ingredients. On the other hand, discouragement, low expectations, and lack of involvement by executives lead to poor employee performance perpetuated by low self-esteem.

The author contributes to the republication of his "classic" article a retrospective commentary outlining his perspective on it 19 years later.

IN GEORGE BERNARD SHAW'S *Pygmalion*, Eliza Doolittle explains:

"You see, really and truly, apart from the things anyone can pick up (the dressing and the proper way of speaking, and so on), the difference between a lady and a flower girl is not how she behaves but how she's treated. I shall always be a flower girl to Professor Higgins because he always treats me as a flower girl and always will; but I know I can be a lady to you because you always treat me as a lady and always will."

Some managers always treat their subordinates in a way that leads to superior performance. But most managers, like Professor Higgins, unintentionally treat their subordinates in a way that leads to lower performance than they are capable of achieving. The way managers treat their subordinates is subtly influenced by what they expect of them. If managers' expectations are high, productivity is likely to be excellent. If their expectations are low, productivity is likely to be poor. It is as though there were a law that caused subordinates' performance to rise or fall to meet managers' expectations.

The powerful influence of one person's expectations on another's behavior has long been recognized by physicians and behavioral scientists and, more recently, by teachers. But heretofore the importance of managerial expectations for individual and group performance has not been widely understood. I have documented this phenomenon in a number of case studies prepared during the past decade for major industrial concerns. (See "Retrospective Commentary," on page 68.) These cases and other evidence available from scientific research now reveal:

Enthusiasm and apathy—both are infectious.

- What managers expect of their subordinates and the way they treat them largely determine their performance and career progress.

- A unique characteristic of superior managers is the ability to create high performance expectations that subordinates fulfill.

- Less effective managers fail to develop similar expectations, and as a consequence, the productivity of their subordinates suffers.

- Subordinates, more often than not, appear to do what they believe they are expected to do.

Impact on Productivity

One of the most comprehensive illustrations of the effect of managerial expectations on productivity is recorded in studies of the organizational experiment undertaken in 1961 by Alfred Oberlander, manager of the Rockaway district office of the Metropolitan Life Insurance Company. He had observed that outstanding insurance agencies grew faster than average or poor agencies and that new insurance agents performed better in outstanding agencies than in average or poor agencies, regardless of their sales aptitude. He decided, therefore, to group his superior agents in one unit to stimulate their performance and to provide a challenging environment in which to introduce new salespeople.

Accordingly, Oberlander assigned his six best agents to work with his best assistant manager, an equal number of average producers to work with an average assistant manager, and the remaining low producers to work with the least able manager. He then asked the superior group to produce two-thirds of the premium volume achieved by the entire agency during the previous year. He describes the results as follows:

"Shortly after this selection had been made, the people in the agency began referring to this select group as a 'superstaff' because of their high esprit de corps in operating so well as a unit. Their production efforts over the first 12 weeks far surpassed our most optimistic expectations . . . proving that groups of people of sound ability can be motivated beyond their apparently normal productive capacities when the problems created by the poor producer are eliminated from the operation.

"Thanks to this fine result, our overall agency performance improved by 40% and it remained at this figure.

"In the beginning of 1962 when, through expansion, we appointed another assistant manager and assigned him a staff, we again used this same concept, arranging the agents once more according to their productive capacity.

"The assistant managers were assigned . . . according to their ability, with the most capable assistant manager receiving the best group, thus playing strength to strength. Our agency overall production again improved by about 25% to 30%, and so this staff arrangement remained in place until the end of the year.

"Now in this year of 1963, we found upon analysis that there were so many agents . . . with a potential of half a million dollars or more that only one staff remained of those people in the agency who were not considered to have any chance of reaching the half-million-dollar mark."

Although the productivity of the "superstaff" improved dramatically, it should be pointed out that the productivity of those in the lowest unit, "who were not considered to have any chance of reaching the half-million-dollar mark," actually declined, and that attrition among them increased. The performance of the superior agents rose to meet their managers' expectations, while that of the weaker ones declined as predicted.

SELF-FULFILLING PROPHECIES

The "average" unit, however, proved to be an anomaly. Although the district manager expected only average performance from this group, its productivity increased significantly. This was because the assistant manager in charge of the group refused to believe that she was less capable than the manager of the superstaff or that the agents in the top group had any greater ability than the agents in her group. She insisted in discussions with her agents that every person in the middle group had greater potential than those in the superstaff, lacking only their years of experience in selling insurance. She stimulated her agents to accept the challenge of outperforming the superstaff. As a result, in each year the middle group increased its productivity by a higher percentage than the superstaff did (although it never attained the dollar volume of the top group).

It is of special interest that the self-image of the manager of the "average" unit did not permit her to accept others' treatment of her as an "average" manager, just as Eliza Doolittle's image of herself as a lady did not permit her to accept others' treatment of her as a flower girl. The assistant manager transmitted her own strong feelings of efficacy to her agents, created mutual expectancy of high performance, and greatly stimulated productivity.

Comparable results occurred when a similar experiment was made at another office of the company. Further confirmation comes from a study of the early managerial success of 49 college graduates who were management-level employees of an operating company of AT&T. David E. Berlew and Douglas T. Hall of the Massachusetts Institute of Technology examined the career progress of these managers over a period of five years and discovered that their relative success, as measured by salary increases and the company's estimate of each one's performance and potential, depended largely on the company's expectations of them.

Salespeople treated by their bosses as "superstaff" try to live up to that image.

The influence of one person's expectations on another's behavior is by no means a business discovery. More than half a century ago, Albert Moll concluded from his clinical experience that subjects behaved as they believed they were expected to. The phenomenon he observed, in which "the prophecy causes its own fulfillment," has recently become a subject of considerable scientific interest. For example:

- In a series of scientific experiments, Robert Rosenthal of Harvard University has demonstrated that a "teacher's expectation for a pupil's intellectual competence can come to serve as an educational self-fulfilling prophecy."

- An experiment in a summer Headstart program for 60 preschoolers compared the performance of pupils under (a) teachers who had been led to expect relatively slow learning by their children, and (b) teachers who had been led to believe that their children had excellent intellectual ability and learning capacity. Pupils of the second group of teachers learned much faster.[1]

Moreover, the healing professions have long recognized that a physician's or psychiatrist's expectations can have a formidable influence on a patient's physical or mental health. What takes place in the minds of the patients and the healers, particularly when they have congruent expectations, may determine the outcome. For instance, the havoc of a doctor's pessimistic prognosis has often been observed. Again, it is well known that the efficacy of a new drug or a new treatment can be greatly influenced by the physician's expectations—a result referred to by the medical profession as a "placebo effect."

PATTERN OF FAILURE

When salespersons are treated by their managers as superpeople, as the superstaff was at the Metropolitan Rockaway district office, they try to live up to that image and do what they know supersalespersons are expected to do. But when the agents with poor productivity records are treated by their managers as *not* having "any chance" of success, as the low producers at Rockaway were, this negative expectation also becomes a managerial self-fulfilling prophecy.

Unsuccessful salespersons have great difficulty maintaining their self-image and self-esteem. In response to low managerial expectations, they typically attempt to prevent additional damage to their egos by avoiding situations that might lead to greater failure. They either reduce the number of sales calls they make or avoid trying to "close" sales when that might result in further painful rejection, or both. Low expectations and damaged egos lead them to behave in a manner that increases the probability of failure, thereby fulfilling their managers' expectations. Let me illustrate:

Not long ago I studied the effectiveness of branch bank managers at a West Coast bank with over 500 branches. The managers who had had their lending authority reduced because of high rates of loss became progressively less effective. To prevent further loss of authority, they turned to making only "safe" loans. This action resulted in losses of business to competing banks and a relative decline in both deposits and profits at their branches. Then, to reverse that decline in deposits and earnings, they often "reached" for loans and became almost irrational in their acceptance of questionable credit risks. Their actions were not so much a matter of poor judgment as an expression of their willingness to take desperate risks in the hope of being able to avoid further damage to their egos and to their careers.

Thus, in response to the low expectations of their supervisors who had reduced their lending authority, they behaved in a manner that led to larger credit losses.

They appeared to do what they believed they were expected to do, and their supervisors' expectations became self-fulfilling prophecies.

Power of Expectations

Managers cannot avoid the depressing cycle of events that flow from low expectations merely by hiding their feelings from subordinates. If managers believe subordinates will perform poorly, it is virtually impossible for them to mask their expectations because the message usually is communicated unintentionally, without conscious action on their part.

Indeed, managers often communicate most when they believe they are communicating least. For instance, when they say nothing—become cold and uncommunicative—it usually is a sign that they are displeased by a subordinate or believe that he or she is hopeless. The silent treatment communicates negative feelings even more effectively, at times, than a tongue-lashing does. What seems to be critical in the communication of expectations is not what the boss says so much as the way he or she behaves. Indifferent and noncommital treatment, more often than not, is the kind of treatment that communicates low expectations and leads to poor performance.

Indifference says to subordinates, "I don't think much of you."

COMMON ILLUSIONS

Managers are more effective in communicating low expectations to their subordinates than in communicating high expectations to them, even though most managers believe exactly the opposite. It usually is astonishingly difficult for them to recognize the clarity with which they transmit negative feelings. To illustrate again:

- The Rockaway district manager vigorously denied that he had communicated low expectations to the agents in the poorest group who, he believed, did not have "any chance" of becoming high producers. Yet the message was clearly received by those agents. A typical case was that of an agent who resigned from the low unit. When the district manager told the agent that he was sorry she was leaving, the agent replied, "No you're not; you're glad." Although the district manager previously had said nothing to her, he had unintentionally communicated his low expectations to his agents through his indifferent manner. Subsequently, the agents who were assigned to the lowest unit interpreted the assignment as equivalent to a request for their resignation.

- One of the company's agency managers established superior, average, and low units, even though he was convinced that he had no superior or outstanding subordinates. "All my assistant managers and agents are either average or incompetent," he explained to the Rockaway district manager. Although he tried to duplicate the Rockaway results, his low opinions of his agents were communicated—not so subtly—to them. As a result, the experiment failed.

Positive feelings, on the other hand, often do not come through clearly enough. Another insurance agency manager copied the organizational changes made at the Rockaway district office, grouping the salespeople she rated highly with the best manager, the average salespeople with an average manager, and so on. Improvement, however, did not result from the move. The Rockaway district manager therefore investigated the situation. He discovered that the assistant manager in charge of the high-performance unit was unaware that his manager considered him to be the best. In fact, he and the other agents doubted that the agency manager really believed there was any difference in their abilities. This agency manager was a stolid, phlegmatic, unemotional woman who treated her agents in a rather pedestrian way. Since high expectations had not been communicated to them, they did not understand the reason for the new organization and could not see any point in it. Clearly, the way managers *treat* subordinates, not the way they organize them, is the key to high expectations and high productivity.

IMPOSSIBLE DREAMS

Managerial expectations must pass the test of reality before they can be translated into performance. To become self-fulfilling prophecies, expectations must be made of sterner stuff than the power of positive thinking or generalized confidence in one's subordinates—helpful as these concepts may be for some other purposes. Subordinates will not be motivated to reach high levels of productivity unless they consider the boss's high expectations realistic and achievable. If they are encouraged to strive for unattainable goals, they eventually give up trying and settle for results that are lower than they are capable of achieving. The experience of a large electrical manufacturing company demonstrates this; the company discovered that production actually declined if production quotas were set too high, because the workers simply stopped trying to meet them. In other words, the practice of "dangling the carrot just beyond the donkey's reach," endorsed by many managers, is not a good motivational device.

Scientific research by David C. McClelland of Harvard University and John W. Atkinson of the University of Michigan has demonstrated that the relationship of motivation to expectancy varies in the form of a bell-shaped curve (See the exhibit below.)[2]

The degree of motivation and effort rises until the expectancy of success reaches 50%, then begins to fall even though the expectancy of success continues to increase. No motivation or response is aroused when the goal is perceived as being either virtually certain or virtually impossible to attain.

Moreover, as Berlew and Hall have pointed out, if subordinates fail to meet performance expectations that are close to their own level of aspirations, they will lower

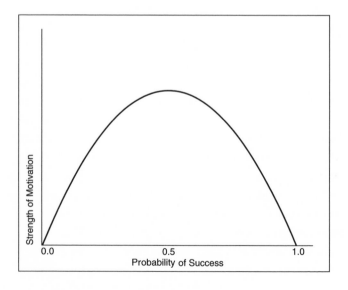

personal performance goals and standards, performance will tend to drop off, and negative attitudes will develop toward the activity or job.[3] It is therefore not surprising that failure of subordinates to meet the unrealistically high expectations of their managers leads to high rates of attrition, either voluntary or involuntary.

SECRET OF SUPERIORITY

Something takes place in the minds of superior managers that does not occur in the minds of those who are less effective. While superior managers are consistently able to create high performance expectations that their subordinates fulfill, weaker managers are not successful in obtaining a similar response. What accounts for the difference?

The answer, in part, seems to be that superior managers have greater confidence than other managers in their own ability to develop the talents of their subordinates. Contrary to what might be assumed, the high expectations of superior managers are based primarily on what they think about themselves—about their own ability to select, train, and motivate their subordinates. What managers believe about themselves subtly influences what they believe about their subordinates, what they expect of them, and how they treat them. If they have confidence in their ability to develop and stimulate them to high levels of performance, they will expect much of them and will treat them with confidence that their expectations will be met. But if they have doubts about their ability to stimulate them, they will expect less of them and will treat them with less confidence.

Stated in another way, the superior managers' record of success and their confidence in their ability give their high expectations credibility. As a consequence, their subordinates accept these expectations as realistic and try hard to achieve them.

The importance of what a manager believes about his or her training and motivational ability is illustrated by "Sweeney's Miracle," a managerial and educational self-fulfilling prophecy.

James Sweeney taught industrial management and psychiatry at Tulane University, and he also was responsible for the operation of the Biomedical Computer Center there. Sweeney believed that he could teach even a poorly educated man to be a capable computer operator. George Johnson, a former hospital porter, became janitor at the computer center; he was chosen by Sweeney to prove his conviction. In the mornings, George Johnson performed his janitorial duties, and in the afternoons Sweeney taught him about computers.

Johnson was learning a great deal about computers when someone at the university concluded that to be a computer operator one had to have a certain I.Q. score. Johnson was tested, and his I.Q. indicated that he would not be able to learn to type, much less operate a computer.

But Sweeney was not convinced. He threatened to quit unless Johnson was permitted to learn to program and operate the computer. Sweeney prevailed, and he is still running the computer center. Johnson is now in charge of the main computer room and is responsible for training new employees to program and operate the computer.[4]

Sweeney's expectations were based on what he believed about his own teaching ability, not on Johnson's learning credentials. What managers believe about their ability to train and motivate subordinates clearly is the foundation on which realistically high managerial expectations are built.

The Critical Early Years

Managerial expectations have their most magical influence on young people. As subordinates mature and gain experience, their self-image gradually hardens, and they begin to see themselves as their career records imply. Their own aspirations and the expectations of their superiors become increasingly controlled by the "reality" of their past performance. It becomes more and more difficult for them and for their managers to generate mutually high expectations unless they have outstanding records.

Incidentally, the same pattern occurs in school. Rosenthal's experiments with educational self-fulfilling prophecies consistently demonstrate that teachers' expectations are more effective in influencing intellectual growth in younger children than in older children. In the lower grade levels, particularly in the first and second grades, the effects of teachers' expectations are dramatic. In the upper grade levels, teachers' prophecies seem to have little effect on children's intellectual growth, although they do affect their motivation and attitude toward school. While the declining influence of teachers' expectations cannot be completely explained, it is reasonable to conclude that younger children are more malleable, have fewer fixed notions about their abilities, and have less well-established reputations in the schools. As they grow, particularly if they are assigned to "tracks" on the basis of their records, as is now often done in public schools, their beliefs about their intellectual ability and their teachers' expectations of them begin to harden and become more resistant to influence by others.

KEY TO FUTURE PERFORMANCE

The early years in a business organization, when young people can be strongly influenced by managerial expectations, are critical in determining future performance and career progress. This is shown by a study at AT&T.

Berlew and Hall found that what the company initially expected of 49 college graduates who were management-level employees was the most critical factor in their subsequent performance and success. The researchers concluded that the correlation between how much a company expects of an employee in the first year and how much that employee contributes during the next five years was "too compelling to be ignored."[5]

Subsequently, the two men studied the career records of 18 college graduates who were hired as management trainees in another of AT&T's operating companies. Again they found that both expectations and performance in the first year correlated consistently with later performance and success.

"Something important is happening in the first year . . . ," Berlew and Hall concluded. "Meeting high company expectations in the critical first year leads to the internalization of positive job attitudes and high standards; these attitudes and standards, in turn, would first lead to and be reinforced by strong performance and success in later years. It should also follow that a new manager who meets the challenge of one highly demanding job will be given subsequently a more demanding job, and his level of contribution will rise as he responds to the company's growing expectations of him. The key . . . is the concept of the first year as a *critical period for learning,* a time when the trainee is uniquely ready to develop or change in the direction of the company's expectations."[6]

MOST INFLUENTIAL BOSS

A young person's first manager is likely to be the most influential in that person's career. If managers are unable or unwilling to develop the skills young employees need to perform effectively, the latter will set lower personal standards than they are capable of achieving, their self-images will be impaired, and they will develop negative attitudes toward jobs, employers, and—in all probability—their own careers in business. Since the chances of building successful careers with these first employers will decline rapidly, the employees will leave, if they have high aspirations, in hope of finding better opportunities. If, on the other hand, early managers help employees achieve maximum potential, they will build the foundations for successful careers.

With few exceptions, the most effective branch managers at a large West Coast bank were mature people in their forties and fifties. The bank's executives explained that it took considerable time for a person to gain the knowledge, experience, and judgment required to handle properly credit risks, customer relations, and employee relations.

One branch manager, however, ranked in the top 10% of the managers in terms of effectiveness (which included branch profit growth, deposit growth, scores on administrative audits, and subjective rankings by superiors), was only 27 years old. This young person had been made a branch manager at 25, and in two years had improved not only the performance of the branch substantially but also developed a younger assistant manager who, in turn, was made a branch manager at 25.

The assistant had had only average grades in college, but in just four years at the bank had been assigned to work with two branch managers who were remarkably effective teachers. The first boss, who was recognized throughout the bank for unusual skill in developing young people, did not believe that it took years to gain the knowledge and skill needed to become an effective banker. After two years, the young person was made assistant manager at a branch headed by another executive, who also was an effective developer of subordinates. Thus it was that the young person, when promoted to head a branch, confidently followed the model of two previous superiors in operating the branch, quickly established a record of outstanding performance, and trained an assistant to assume responsibility early.

For confirming evidence of the crucial role played by a person's first bosses, let us turn to selling, since performance in this area is more easily measured than in most managerial areas. Consider the following investigations:

- In a study of the careers of 100 insurance salespeople who began work with either highly competent or less-than-competent agency managers, the Life Insurance Agency Management Association found that those with average sales-aptitude test scores were nearly five times as likely to succeed under managers with good performance records as under managers with poor records, and those with superior sales aptitude scores were found to be twice as likely to succeed under high-performing managers as under low-performing managers.[7]

- The Metropolitan Life Insurance Company determined in 1960 that differences in the productivity of new insurance agents who had equal sales aptitudes could be accounted for only by differences in the ability of managers in the offices to which they were assigned. Agents whose productivity was high in relation to their aptitude test scores invariably were employed in offices that had production records among the top third in the company. Conversely, those whose productivity was low in relation to their test scores typically were in the least successful offices. After analyzing all the factors that might have accounted for these variations, the company concluded that differences in the performance of new agents were due primarily to differences in the "proficiency in sales training and direction" of the local managers.[8]

- A study I conducted of the performance of automobile salespeople in Ford dealerships in New England revealed that superior salespersons were concentrated in a few outstanding dealerships. For instance, 10 of the top 15 salespeople in New England were in 3 (out of approximately 200) of the dealerships in this region, and 5 of the top 15 people were in one highly successful dealership. Yet 4 of these people previously had worked for other dealers without achieving outstanding sales records. There was little doubt that the training and motivational skills of managers in the outstanding dealerships were critical.

ASTUTE SELECTION

While success in business sometimes appears to depend on the luck of the draw, more than luck is involved when a young person is selected by a superior manager. Successful managers do not pick their subordinates at random or by the toss of a coin. They are careful to select only those who they "know" will succeed. As Metropolitan's Rockaway district manager, Alfred Oberlander, insisted: "Every man or woman who starts with us is going to be a top-notch life insurance agent, or he or she would not have been asked to join the team."

When pressed to explain how they "know" whether a person will be successful, superior managers usually end up by saying something like, "The qualities are intangible, but I know them when I see them." They have difficulty being explicit because their selection process is intuitive and is based on interpersonal intelligence that is difficult to describe. The key seems to be that they are able to identify subordinates with whom they can probably work effectively—people with whom they are compatible and whose body chemistry agrees with their own. They make mistakes, of course. But they "give up" on a subordinate slowly because that means "giving up" on themselves—on their judgment and ability in selecting, training, and motivating people. Less effective managers select subordinates more quickly and give up on them more easily, believing that the inadequacy is that of the subordinate, not of themselves.

Developing Young People

Observing that his company's research indicates that "initial corporate expectations for performance (with real responsibility) mold subsequent expectations and behavior," R.W. Walters, Jr., director of college employment at AT&T, contends that "initial bosses of new college hires must be the best in the organization."[9] Unfortunately, however, most companies practice exactly the opposite.

Rarely do new graduates work closely with experienced middle managers or upper-level executives. Normally they are bossed by first-line managers who tend to be the least experienced and least effective in the organization. While there are exceptions, first-line managers generally are either "old pros" who have been judged as lacking competence for higher levels of responsibility, or they are younger people who are making the transition from "doing" to "managing." Often these managers lack the knowledge and skill required to develop the productive capabilities of their subordinates. As a consequence, many college graduates begin their careers in business under the worst possible circumstances. Since they know their abilities are not being developed or used, they quite naturally soon become negative toward their jobs, employers, and business careers.

Although most top executives have not yet diagnosed the problem, industry's greatest challenge by far is to rectify the underdevelopment, underutilization, and ineffective management and use of its most valuable resource—its young managerial and professional talent.

DISILLUSION AND TURNOVER

The problem posed to corporate management is underscored by the sharply rising rates of attrition among young managerial and professional personnel. Turnover among managers one to five years out of college is almost twice as high now as it was a decade ago, and five times as high as two decades ago. Three out of five companies surveyed by *Fortune* magazine in the fall of 1968 reported that turnover rates among young managers and professionals were higher than five years ago.[10] While the high level of economic activity and the shortage of skilled personnel have made job-hopping easier, the underlying causes of high attrition, I am convinced, are underdevelopment and underutilization of a work force that has high career aspirations.

The problem can be seen in its extreme form in the excessive attrition rates of college and university graduates who begin their careers in sales positions. Whereas the average company loses about 50% of its new college and university graduates within three to five years, attrition rates as high as 40% in the *first* year are common among college graduates who accept sales positions in the average company. This attrition stems primarily, in my opinion, from the failure of first-line managers to teach new college recruits what they need to know to be effective sales representatives.

As we have seen, young people who begin their careers working for less-than-competent sales managers are likely to have records of low productivity. When rebuffed by their customers and considered by their managers to have little potential for success, the young people naturally have great difficulty in maintaining their self-esteem. Soon they find little personal satisfaction in their jobs and, to avoid further loss of self-respect, leave their employers for jobs that look more promising. Moreover, as reports about the high turnover and disillusionment of those who embarked on sales careers filter back to college campuses, new graduates become increasingly reluctant to take jobs in sales.

Thus ineffective first-line sales management sets off a sequence of events that ends with college and university graduates avoiding careers in selling. To a lesser extent, the same pattern is duplicated in other functions of business, as evidenced by the growing trend of college graduates to pursue careers in "more meaningful" occupations, such as teaching and government service.

A serious "generation gap" between bosses and subordinates is another significant cause of breakdown. Many managers resent the abstract, academic language and narrow rationalization characteristically used by recent graduates. As one manager expressed it to me, "For God's sake, you need a lexicon even to talk with these kids." Nondegreed managers often are particularly resentful, perhaps because they feel threatened by the bright young people with book-learned knowledge that they do not understand.

For whatever reason, the "generation gap" in many companies is eroding managerial expectations of new college graduates. For instance, I know of a survey of management attitudes in one of the nation's largest companies that revealed that 54% of its first-line and second-line managers believed that new college recruits were "not as good as they were five years ago." Since what managers expect of subordinates influences the way they treat them, it is understandable that new graduates often develop negative attitudes toward their jobs and their employers. Clearly, low managerial expectations and hostile attitudes are not the basis for effective management of new people entering business.

INDUSTRY HAS NOT DEVELOPED effective first-line managers fast enough to meet its needs. As a consequence, many companies are underdeveloping their most valuable resource—talented young men and women. They are incurring heavy attrition costs and contributing to the negative attitudes young people often have about careers in business.

For top executives in industry who are concerned with the productivity of their organizations and the careers of young employees, the challenge is clear: to speed the development of managers who will treat subordinates in ways that lead to high performance and career satisfaction. Managers not only shape the expectations and productivity of their subordinates but also influence their attitudes toward their jobs and themselves. If managers are unskilled, they leave scars on the careers of young people, cut deeply into their self-esteem, and distort their image of themselves as human beings. But if they are skillful and have high expectations, subordinates' self-confidence will grow, their capabilities will develop, and their productivity will be high. More often than one realizes, the manager is Pygmalion.

We are all like Eliza Doolittle—we behave according to how we're treated.

Retrospective Commentary

SELF-FULFILLING MANAGERIAL PROPHECIES WERE a bit mysterious when I documented the phenomenon 19 years ago. At that time, the powerful influence of managers' expectations on the development, motivation, and performance of their subordinates was not widely understood. Since then, however, the "Pygmalion effect" has become well known.

Recent research has confirmed that effective leaders have the ability to create high performance expectations that their employees fulfill. Every manager should understand, therefore, how the Pygmalion effect works.

What managers think about themselves and their abilities, as I explained in "Pygmalion in Management," is crucial to their effectiveness in creating self-fulfilling prophecies. Warren Bennis and Burt Nanus recently reached a similar conclusion after conducting some 90 interviews with CEOs and top public administrators. They wrote: "Our study of effective leaders strongly suggested that a key factor was . . . what we're calling . . . positive self-regard. . . . Positive self-regard seems to exert its force by creating in others a sense of confidence and high expectations, not very different from the fabled Pygmalion effect."[11]

The way managers develop confidence in their abilities and transmit their feelings of efficacy to their employees is illustrated by the success of Lee A. Iacocca of Chrysler—whom, interestingly, Bennis and Nanus used as a model for their theory of leadership. Iacocca's self-assurance can be traced to his prior success as president of Ford. His subsequent prophecy that Chrysler would be saved was accepted as credible by Chrysler's employees because they saw him as a competent automobile executive. They tried hard to meet his expectations and "behaved as they believed they were expected to," which my article indicated would be normal under the circumstances.

It is highly unlikely, however, that Iacocca could have saved Chrysler if he had been an industry outsider who needed two or three years to learn the automotive business. If he had been an outsider, he could not have moved decisively to do what needed to be done, nor could he have created a strong sense of confidence and high expectations among Chrysler's employees. His success was due to his experience and competence. It is doubtful that a prophecy by a less-qualified executive would have been self-fulfilling. So the message for managers is this: to be a Pygmalion, you must acquire the industry knowledge and job skills required to be confident of your high expectations and to make them credible to your employees.

Your organization can help identify the knowledge and skills you need to perform your job effectively. Your supervisors can give you assignments that will spur your development. But you must assume responsibility for your own development and career growth.

A word of caution may be in order, however. As I explained in my article, managers often unintentionally communicate low expectations to their subordinates, even though they believe otherwise. When they communicate low expectations, they become "negative" Pygmalions who undermine the self-confidence of their employees and reduce their effectiveness. Managers must be extremely sensitive, therefore, to their own behavior and its impact on their subordinates. They must guard against treating their employees in ways that lower their feelings of efficacy and self-esteem and are unproductive.

If I were writing "Pygmalion in Management" today, I might focus more attention on the problems of the negative Pygmalions because there are more of them than positive Pygmalions in U.S. industry. But the dark side of the Pygmalion effect is distressing, and I prefer to think about the bright side. It is a hopeful concept that can help all managers become more effective.

The difference between employees who perform well and those who perform poorly is not how they are paid but how they are treated. All managers can learn how to treat their employees in ways that will lead to mutual expectations of superior performance. The most effective managers always do.

Notes

1. The Rosenthal and Headstart studies are cited in Robert Rosenthal and Lenore Jacobson, *Pygmalion in the Classroom* (New York: Holt, Rinehart, and Winston, Inc., 1968), p. 11.

2. See John W. Atkinson, "Motivational Determinants of Risk-Taking Behavior," *Psychological Review*, vol. 64, no. 6, 1957, p. 365.

3. David E. Berlew and Douglas T. Hall, "The Socialization of Managers: Effects of Expectations on Performance," *Administrative Science Quarterly*, September 1966, p. 208.

4. See Rosenthal and Jacobson, *Pygmalion in the Classroom*, p. 3.

5. Berlew and Hall, "The Socialization of Managers," p. 221.

6. David E. Berlew and Douglas T. Hall, "Some Determinants of Early Managerial Success," Alfred P. Sloan School of Management Organization Research Program #81–64 (Cambridge: MIT, 1964), p. 13.

7. Robert T. Davis, "Sales Management in the Field," HBR January–February 1958, p. 91.

8. Alfred A. Oberlander, "The Collective Conscience in Recruiting," address to Life Insurance Agency Management Association annual meeting, Chicago, Illinois, 1963, p. 5.

9. "How to Keep the Go-Getters," *Nation's Business*, June 1966, p. 74.

10. Robert C. Albrook, "Why It's Harder to Keep Good Executives," *Fortune*, November 1968, p. 137.

11. Reported in their book *Leaders* (New York: Harper & Row, 1985).

Originally published in September–October 1988
Reprint 88509

Six Dangerous Myths About Pay

JEFFREY PFEFFER

Executive Summary

EVERY DAY, EXECUTIVES MAKE DECISIONS about pay, and they do so in a landscape that's shifting. As more and more companies base less of their compensation on straight salary and look to other financial options, managers are bombarded with advice about the best approaches to take.

Unfortunately, much of that advice is wrong. Indeed, much of the conventional wisdom and public discussion about pay today is misleading, incorrect, or both. The result is that businesspeople are adopting wrongheaded notions about how to pay people and why. In particular, they are subscribing to six dangerous myths about pay.

- Myth #1: labor rates are the same as labor costs.
- Myth #2: cutting labor rates will lower labor costs.

- Myth #3: labor costs represent a large portion of a company's total costs.

- Myth #4: keeping labor costs low creates a potent and sustainable competitive edge.

- Myth #5: individual incentive pay improves performance.

- Myth #6: people work primarily for the money.

The author explains why these myths are so pervasive, shows where they go wrong, and suggests how leaders might think more productively about compensation.

With increasing frequency, the author says, he sees managers harming their organizations by buying into—and acting on—these myths. Those that do, he warns, are probably doomed to endless tinkering with pay that at the end of the day will accomplish little but cost a lot.

---

*C*onsider two groups of steel minimills. One group pays an average hourly wage of $18.07. The second pays an average of $21.52 an hour. Assuming that other direct-employment costs, such as benefits, are the same for the two groups, which group has the higher labor costs?

An airline is seeking to compete in the low-cost, low-frills segment of the U.S. market where, for obvious reasons, labor productivity and efficiency are crucial for competitive success. The company pays virtually no one on the basis of individual merit or performance. Does it stand a chance of success?

A company that operates in an intensely competitive segment of the software industry does not pay its sales force on commission. Nor does it pay individual bonuses or offer stock options or phantom stock, common incen-

tives in an industry heavily dependent on attracting and retaining scarce programming talent. Would you invest in this company?

Every day, organizational leaders confront decisions about pay. Should they adjust the company's compensation system to encourage some set of behaviors? Should they retain consultants to help them implement a performance-based pay system? How large a raise should they authorize?

In general terms, these kinds of questions come down to four decisions about compensation:

- how much to pay employees;

- how much emphasis to place on financial compensation as a part of the total reward system;

- how much emphasis to place on attempting to hold down the rate of pay; and

- whether to implement a system of individual incentives to reward differences in performance and productivity and, if so, how much emphasis to place on these incentives.

For leaders, there can be no delegation of these matters. Everyone knows decisions about pay are important. For one thing, they help establish a company's culture by rewarding the business activities, behaviors, and values that senior managers hold dear. Senior management at Quantum, the disk drive manufacturer in Milpitas, California, for example, demonstrates its commitment to teamwork by placing all employees, from the CEO to hourly workers, on the same

Managers are bombarded with advice about pay. Unfortunately, much of that advice is wrong.

bonus plan, tracking everyone by the same measure—in this case, return on total capital.

Compensation is also a concept and practice very much in flux. Compensation is becoming more variable as companies base a greater proportion of it on stock options and bonuses and a smaller proportion on base salary, not only for executives but also for people further and further down the hierarchy. As managers make organization-defining decisions about pay systems, they do so in a shifting landscape while being bombarded with advice about the best routes to stable ground.

Unfortunately, much of that advice is wrong. Indeed, much of the conventional wisdom and public discussion about pay today is misleading, incorrect, or sometimes both at the same time. The result is that businesspeople end up adopting wrongheaded notions about how to pay people and why. They believe in six dangerous myths about pay—fictions about compensation that have somehow come to be seen as the truth. (See "Truth and Consequences: The Six Dangerous Myths About Compensation," on page 97.)

Do you think you have managed to avoid these myths? Let's see how you answered the three questions that open this article. If you said the second set of steel minimills had higher labor costs, you fell into the common trap of confusing labor *rates* with labor *costs*. That is Myth #1: that labor rates and labor costs are the same thing. But how different they really are. The second set of minimills paid its workers at a rate of $3.45 an hour more than the first. But according to data collected by Fairfield University Professor Jeffrey Arthur, its labor costs were much lower because the productivity of the mills was higher. The second set of mills actually required 34% fewer labor hours to produce a ton of steel than the first set and also generated 63% less scrap. The second set of mills could have raised workers' pay rate by 19% and still had lower labor costs.

Connected to the first myth are three more myths that draw on the same logic. When managers believe that labor costs and labor rates are the same thing, they also tend to believe that they can cut labor costs by cutting labor rates. That's Myth #2. Again, this leaves out the important matter of productivity. I may replace my $2,000-a-week engineers with ones that earn $500 a week, but my costs may skyrocket because the new, lower-paid employees are inexperienced, slow, and less capable. In that case, I would have increased my costs by cutting my rates.

Managers who mix up labor rates and labor costs also tend to accept Myth #3: that labor costs are a significant portion of total costs. Sometimes, that's true. It is, for example, at accounting and consulting firms. But the ratio of labor costs to total costs varies widely in different industries and companies. And even where it is true, it's not as important as many managers believe. Those who swallow Myth #4—that low labor costs are a potent competitive strategy—may neglect other, more effective ways of competing, such as through quality, service, delivery, and innovation. In reality, low labor costs are a slippery way to compete and perhaps the least sustainable competitive advantage there is.

Those of you who believed that the airline trying to compete in the low-cost, low-frills segment of the U.S. market would not succeed without using individual incentives succumbed to Myth #5: that the most effective way to motivate people to work productively is through individual incentive compensation. But Southwest Airlines has never used such a system, and it is the cost and productivity leader in its industry. Southwest is not alone, but still it takes smart, informed managers to buck the trend of offering individual rewards.

Would you have invested in the computer software company that didn't offer its people bonuses, stock options, or other financial incentives that could make them millionaires? You should have because it has succeeded mightily, growing over the past 21 years at a compound annual rate of more than 25%. The company is the SAS Institute of Cary, North Carolina. Today it is the largest privately held company in the software industry, with 1997 revenues of some $750 million.

Rather than emphasize pay, SAS has achieved an unbelievably low turnover rate below 4%—in an industry where the norm is closer to 20%—by offering intellectually engaging work; a family-friendly environment that features exceptional benefits; and the opportunity to work with fun, interesting people using state-of-the-art equipment.

In short, SAS has escaped Myth #6: that people work primarily for money. SAS, operating under the opposite assumption, demonstrates otherwise. In the last three years, the company has lost *none* of its 20 North American district sales managers. How many software companies do you know could make that statement, even about the last three months?

Every day, I see managers harming their organizations by believing in these myths about pay. What I want to do in these following pages is explore some factors that help account for why the myths are so pervasive, present some evidence to disprove their underlying assumptions, and suggest how leaders might think more productively and usefully about the important issue of pay practices in their organizations.

Why the Myths Exist

On October 10, 1997, the *Wall Street Journal* published an article expressing surprise that a "contrarian Motorola" had chosen to build a plant in Germany to make cellular phones despite the notoriously high "cost" of German labor. The *Journal* is not alone in framing business decisions about pay in this way. The *Economist* has also written articles about high German labor "costs," citing as evidence labor rates (including fringe benefits) of more than $30 per hour. The semantic confusion of labor rates with labor costs, endemic in business journalism and everyday discussion, leads managers to see the two as equivalent. And when the two seem equivalent, the associated myths about labor costs seem to make sense, too. But, of course, labor rates and labor costs simply aren't the same thing. A labor rate is total salary divided by time worked. But labor costs take productivity into account. That's how the second set of minimills managed to have lower labor costs than the mills with the lower wages. They made more steel, and they made it faster and better.

Another reason why the confusion over costs and rates persists is that labor rates are a convenient target for managers who want to make an impact. Labor rates are highly visible, and it's easy to compare the rates you pay with those paid by your competitors or with those paid in other parts of the world. In addition, labor rates often appear to be a company's most malleable financial variable. It seems a lot quicker and easier to cut wages than to control costs in other ways, like reconfiguring manufacturing processes, changing corporate culture, or altering product design. Because labor costs appear to be the lever closest at hand, managers mistakenly assume it is the one that has the most leverage.

For the myths that individual incentive pay drives creativity and productivity, and that people are primarily motivated by money, we have economic theory to blame. More specifically, we can blame the economic model of human behavior widely taught in business schools and held to be true in the popular press. This model presumes that behavior is rational—driven by the best information available at the time and designed to maximize the individual's self-interest. According to this model, people take jobs and decide how much effort to expend in those jobs based on their expected financial return. If pay is not contingent on performance, the theory goes, individuals will not devote sufficient attention and energy to their jobs.

Additional problems arise from such popular economic concepts as agency theory (which contends that there are differences in preference and perspective between owners and those who work for them) and transaction-cost economics (which tries to identify which transactions are best organized by markets and which by hierarchies). Embedded in both concepts is the idea that individuals not only pursue self-interest but do so on occasion with guile and opportunism. Thus agency theory suggests that employees have different objectives than their employers and, moreover, have opportunities to misrepresent information and divert resources to their personal use. Transaction-cost theory suggests that people will make false or empty threats and promises to get better deals from one another.

All of these economic models portray work as hard and aversive—implying that the only way people can be induced to work is through some combination of rewards and sanctions. As professor James N. Baron of Stanford Business School has written, "The image of workers in these models is somewhat akin to Newton's first law of motion: employees remain in a state of rest unless compelled to change that state by a stronger force impressed upon them—namely, an optimal labor contract."

Similarly, the language of economics is filled with terms such as *shirking* and *free riding*. Language is powerful, and as Robert Frank, himself an economist, has noted, theories of human behavior become self-fulfilling. We act on the basis of these theories, and through our own actions produce in others the behavior we expect. If we believe people will work hard only if specifically rewarded for doing so, we will provide contingent rewards and thereby condition people to work only when they are rewarded. If we expect people to be untrustworthy, we will closely monitor and control them and by doing so will signal that they can't be trusted— an expectation that they will most likely confirm for us.

So self-reinforcing are these ideas that you almost have to avoid mainstream business to get away from them. Perhaps that's why several companies known to be strongly committed to managing through trust, mutual respect, and true decentralization—such as AES Corporation, Lincoln Electric, the Men's Wearhouse, the SAS Institute, ServiceMaster, Southwest Airlines, and Whole Foods

It's simpler for managers to tinker with compensation than to change the company's culture.

Market—tend to avoid recruiting at conventional business schools.

There's one last factor that helps perpetuate all these myths: the compensation-consulting industry. Unfortunately, that industry has a number of perverse incentives to keep these myths alive.

First, although some of these consulting firms have recently broadened their practices, compensation remains their bread and butter. Suggesting that an organization's performance can be improved in some way other than by tinkering with the pay system may be empirically correct but is probably too selfless a behavior to expect from these firms.

Second, if it's simpler for managers to tinker with the compensation system than to change an organization's culture, the way work is organized, and the level of trust and respect the system displays, it's even easier for consultants. Thus both the compensation consultants and their clients are tempted by the apparent speed and ease with which reward-system solutions can be implemented.

Third, to the extent that changes in pay systems bring their own new predicaments, the consultants will continue to have work solving the problems that the tinkering has caused in the first place.

From Myth to Reality: A Look at the Evidence

The media are filled with accounts of companies attempting to reduce their labor costs by laying off people, moving production to places where labor rates are lower, freezing wages, or some combination of the above. In the early 1990s, for instance, Ford decided not to award merit raises to its white-collar workers as part

of a new cost-cutting program. And in 1997, General
Motors endured a series of highly publicized strikes over
the issue of outsourcing. GM wanted to move more of its
work to nonunion, presumably lower-wage, suppliers to
reduce its labor costs and become more profitable.

Ford's and GM's decisions were driven by the myths
that labor rates and labor costs are the same thing, and
that labor costs constitute a significant portion of total
costs. Yet hard evidence to support those contentions is
slim. New United Motor Manufacturing, the joint venture between Toyota and General Motors based in Fre-
mont, California, paid the highest wage in the automobile industry when it began operations in the mid-1980s,
and it also offered a guarantee of secure employment.
With productivity some 50% higher than at comparable
GM plants, the venture could afford to pay 10% more
and still come out ahead.

Yet General Motors apparently did not learn the lesson that what matters is not pay rate but productivity.
In May 1996, as GM was preparing to confront the union
over the issue of outsourcing, the "Harbour Report," the
automobile industry's bible of comparative efficiency,
published some interesting data suggesting that General
Motors' problems had little to do with labor rates. As
reported in the *Wall Street Journal* at the time, the
report showed that it took General Motors some 46
hours to assemble a car, while it took Ford just 37.92
hours, Toyota 29.44, and Nissan only 27.36. As a way of
attacking cost problems, officials at General Motors
should have asked why they needed 21% more hours
than Ford to accomplish the same thing or why GM was
some 68% less efficient than Nissan.

For more evidence of how reality really looks, consider the machine tool industry. Many of its senior managers have been particularly concerned with low-cost

foreign competition, believing that the cost advantage has come from the lower labor rates available offshore. But for machine tool companies that stop fixating on labor rates and focus instead on their overall management system and manufacturing processes, there are great potential returns. Cincinnati Milacron, a company that had virtually surrendered the market for low-end machine tools to Asian competitors by the mid-1980s, overhauled its assembly process, abolished its stockroom, and reduced job categories from seven to one. Without any capital investment, those changes in the production process reduced labor hours by 50%, and the company's productivity is now higher than its competitors' in Taiwan.

Even U.S. apparel manufacturers lend support to the argument that labor costs are not the be-all and end-all of profitability. Companies in this industry are generally obsessed with finding places where hourly wages are low. But the cost of direct labor needed to manufacture a pair of jeans is actually only about 15% of total costs, and even the direct labor involved in producing a man's suit is only about $12.50.[1]

Compelling evidence also exists to dispute the myth that competing on labor costs will create any sustainable advantage. Let's start close to home. One day, I arrived at a large discount store with a shopping list. Having the good fortune to actually find a sales associate, I asked him where I could locate the first item on my list. "I don't know," he replied. He gave a similar reply when queried about the second item. A glance at the long list I was holding brought the confession that because of high employee turnover, the young man had been in the store only a few hours himself. What is that employee worth to the store? Not only can't he sell the merchandise, he can't even find it! Needless to say, I wasn't able to purchase everything on my list because I got tired of looking and gave up. And I haven't returned since. Companies that compete on cost alone eventually bump into consumers like me. It's no accident that Wal-Mart combines its low-price strategy with friendly staff members greeting people at the door and works assiduously to keep turnover low.

Another example of a company that understands the limits of competing solely on labor costs is the Men's Wearhouse, the enormously successful off-price retailer of tailored men's clothing. The company operates in a fiercely competitive industry in which growth is possible primarily by taking sales from competitors, and price wars are intense. Still, less than 15% of the company's staff is part-time, wages are higher than the industry average, and the company engages in extensive training. All these policies defy conventional wisdom for the retailing industry. But the issue isn't what the Men's Wearhouse's employees cost, it's what they can do: sell very effectively because of their product knowledge and sales skills. Moreover, by keeping inventory losses and employee turnover low, the company saves money on shrinkage and hiring. Companies that miss this point— that costs, particularly labor costs, aren't everything— often overlook ways of succeeding that competitors can't readily copy.

Evidence also exists that challenges the myth about the effectiveness of individual incentives. This evidence, however, has done little to stem the tide of individual merit pay. A survey of the pay practices of the *Fortune* 1,000 reported that between 1987 and 1993, the proportion of companies using individual incentives for at least 20% of their workforce increased from 38% to 50% while the proportion of companies using profit sharing—a more collective reward—decreased from 45% to 43%. Between 1981 and 1990, the proportion of retail salespeople that were paid solely on straight salary, with no commission, declined from 21% to 7%. And this trend toward individual incentive compensation is not confined to the United States. A study of pay practices at plants in the United Kingdom reported that the proportion using some form of merit pay had increased every year since 1986 such that by 1990 it had reached 50%.[2]

Despite the evident popularity of this practice, the problems with individual merit pay are numerous and well documented. It has been shown to undermine teamwork, encourage employees to focus on the short term, and lead people to link compensation to political skills and ingratiating personalities rather than to performance. Indeed, those are among the reasons why W. Edwards Deming and other quality experts have argued strongly against using such schemes.

Most merit-pay systems share two attributes: they absorb vast amounts of management time and make everybody unhappy.

Consider the results of several studies. One carefully designed study of a performance-contingent pay plan at 20 Social Security Administration offices found that merit pay had no effect on office performance. Even though the merit pay plan was contingent on a number of objective indicators, such as the time taken to settle claims and the accuracy of claims processing, employees exhibited no difference in performance after the merit pay plan was introduced as part of a reform of civil service pay practices. Contrast that study with another that examined the elimination of a piecework system and its replacement by a more group-oriented compensation system at a manufacturer of exhaust system components. There, grievances decreased, product quality increased almost tenfold, and perceptions of teamwork and concern for performance all improved.[3]

Surveys conducted by various consulting companies that specialize in management and compensation also reveal the problems and dissatisfaction with individual merit pay. For instance, a study by the consulting firm William M. Mercer reported that 73% of the responding companies had made major changes to their perfomance-management plans in the preceding two years, as they experimented with different ways to tie pay to individual performance. But 47% reported that their employees found the systems neither fair nor sensible, and 51% of the employees said that the performance-management system provided little value to the company. No wonder Mercer concluded that most individual merit or performance-based pay plans share two attributes: they absorb vast amounts of management time and resources, and they make everybody unhappy.

One concern about paying on a more group-oriented basis is the so-called free-rider problem, the worry that people will not work hard because they know that if rewards are based on collective performance and their colleagues make the effort, they will share in those rewards regardless of the level of their individual efforts. But there are two reasons why organizations should not be reluctant to design such collective pay systems.

First, much to the surprise of people who have spent too much time reading economics, empirical evidence from numerous studies indicates that the extent of free riding is quite modest. For instance, one comprehensive review reported that "under the conditions described by

the theory as leading to free riding, people often cooperate instead."[4]

Second, individuals do not make decisions about how
much effort to expend in a social vacuum; they are influenced by peer pressure and the social relations they have
with their workmates. This social influence is potent,
and although it may be somewhat stronger in smaller
groups, it can be a force mitigating against free riding
even in large organizations. As one might expect, then,
there is evidence that organizations paying on a more
collective basis, such as through profit sharing or gain
sharing, outperform those that don't.

Sometimes, individual pay schemes go so far as to
affect customers. Sears was forced to eliminate a commission system at its automobile repair stores in California when officials found widespread evidence of consumer fraud. Employees, anxious to meet quotas and
earn commissions on repair sales, were selling unneeded
services to unsuspecting customers. Similarly, in 1992,
the *Wall Street Journal* reported that Highland Superstores, an electronics and appliance retailer, eliminated
commissions because they had encouraged such aggressive behavior on the part of salespeople that customers
were alienated.

Enchantment with individual merit pay reflects not
only the belief that people won't work effectively if they
are not rewarded for
their individual efforts
but also the related view
that the road to solving
organizational problems
is largely paved with
adjustments to pay and measurement practices. Consider again the data from the Mercer survey: nearly

> **People seek an enjoyable
> work environment, one
> where work is not a four-
> letter word.**

three-quarters of all the companies surveyed had made *major* changes to their pay plans in just the past two years. That's tinkering on a grand scale. Or take the case of Air Products and Chemicals of Allentown, Pennsylvania. When on October 23, 1996, the company reported mediocre sales and profits, the stock price declined from the low $60s to the high $50s. Eight days later, the company announced a new set of management-compensation and stock-ownership initiatives designed to reassure Wall Street that management cared about its shareholders and was demonstrating that concern by changing compensation arrangements. The results were dramatic. On the day of the announcement, the stock price went up 1¼ points, and the next day it rose an additional 4¾ points. By November 29, Air Products' stock had gone up more than 15%. According to Value Line, this rise was an enthusiastic reaction by investors to the new compensation system. No wonder managers are so tempted to tamper with pay practices!

But as Bill Strusz, director of corporate industrial relations at Xerox in Rochester, New York, has said, if managers seeking to improve performance or solve organizational problems use compensation as the only lever, they will get two results: nothing will happen, and they will spend a lot of money. That's because people want more out of their jobs than just money. Numerous surveys—even of second-year M.B.A. students, who frequently graduate with large amounts of debt—indicate that money is far from the most important factor in choosing a job or remaining in one.

Why has the SAS Institute had such low turnover in the software industry despite its tight labor market? When asked this question, employees said they were motivated by SAS's unique perks—plentiful opportunities to work with the latest and most up-to-date equipment and the ease with which they could move back and forth between being a manager and being an individual contributor. They also cited how much variety there was in the projects they worked on, how intelligent and nice the people they worked with were, and how much the organization cared for and appreciated them. Of course, SAS pays competitive salaries, but in an industry in which people have the opportunity to become millionaires through stock options by moving to a competitor, the key to retention is SAS's culture, not its monetary rewards.

I would not necessarily say that external rewards backfire, but they do create their own problems.

People seek, in a phrase, an enjoyable work environment. That's what AES, the Men's Wearhouse, SAS, and Southwest have in common. One of the core values at each company is *fun*. When a colleague and I wrote a business school case on Southwest, we asked some of the employees, a number of whom had been offered much more money to work elsewhere, why they stayed. The answer we heard repeatedly was that they knew what the other environments were like, and they would rather be at a place, as one employee put it, where work is not a four-letter word. This doesn't mean work has to be easy. As an AES employee noted, fun means working in a place where people can use their gifts and skills and can work with others in an atmosphere of mutual respect.

There is a great body of literature on the effect of large external rewards on individuals' intrinsic motivation. The literature argues that extrinsic rewards diminish intrinsic motivation and, moreover, that large extrinsic rewards can actually decrease performance in tasks that require creativity and innovation. I would not necessarily go so far as to say that external rewards backfire, but they certainly create their own problems. First, people receiving such rewards can reduce their own motivation through a trick of self-perception, figuring, "I must not like the job if I have to be paid so much to do it" or "I make so much, I must be doing it for the money." Second, they undermine their own loyalty or performance by reacting against a sense of being controlled, thinking something like, "I will show the company that I can't be controlled just through money."

Many executives spend too much time thinking about compensation when other managerial tools work just as well—or better.

But most important, to my mind, is the logic in the idea that any organization believing it can solve its attraction, retention, and motivation problems solely by its compensation system is probably not spending as much time and effort as it should on the work environment—on defining its jobs, on creating its culture, and on making work fun and meaningful. It is a question of time and attention, of scarce managerial resources. The time and attention spent managing the reward system are not available to devote to other aspects of the work environment that in the end may be much more critical to success.

Some Advice About Pay

Since I have traipsed you through a discussion of what's wrong with the way most companies approach compensation, let me now offer some advice about how to get it right.

The first, and perhaps most obvious, suggestion is
that managers would do well to keep the difference
between labor rates and
If you could reliably   labor costs straight. In
measure and reward   doing so, remember that
individual contributions,   only labor costs—and
organizations wouldn't   not labor rates—are the
be needed.   basis for competition,
and that labor costs may
not be a major component of total costs. In any event,
managers should remember that the issue is not just
what you pay people, but also what they produce.

To combat the myth about the effectiveness of individual performance pay, managers should see what happens when they include a large dose of collective
rewards in their employees' compensation package. The
more aggregated the unit used to measure performance,
the more reliably performance can be assessed. One can
tell pretty accurately how well an organization, or even a
subunit, has done with respect to sales, profits, quality,
productivity, and the like. Trying to parcel out who,
specifically, was responsible for exactly how much of
that productivity, quality, or sales is frequently much
more difficult or even impossible. As Herbert Simon, the
Nobel-prize-winning economist, has recognized, people
in organizations are interdependent, and therefore organizational results are the consequence of collective
behavior and performance. If you could reliably and easily measure and reward individual contributions, you
probably would not need an organization at all as everyone would enter markets solely as individuals.

In the typical individual-based merit pay system, the
boss works with a raise budget that's some percentage of
the total salary budget for the unit. It's inherently a zero-

sum process: the more I get in my raise, the less is left for my colleagues. So the worse my workmates perform, the happier I am because I know I will look better by comparison. A similar dynamic can occur across organizational units in which competition for a fixed bonus pool discourages people from sharing best practices and learning from employees in other parts of the organization. In November 1995, for example, *Fortune* magazine reported that at Lantech, a manufacturer of packaging machinery in Louisville, Kentucky, individual incentives caused such intense rivalry that the chairman of the company, Pat Lancaster, said, "I was spending 95% of my time on conflict resolution instead of on how to serve our customers."

Managers can fight the myth that people are primarily motivated by money by de-emphasizing pay and not portraying it as the main thing you get from working at a particular company. How? Consider the example of Tandem Computer which, in the years before it was acquired by Compaq, would not even tell you your salary before expecting you to accept a job. If you asked, you would be told that Tandem paid good, competitive salaries. The company had a simple philosophy—if you came for money, you would leave for money, and Tandem wanted employees who were there because they liked the work, the culture, and the people, not something—money—that every company could offer. Emphasizing pay as the primary reward encourages people to come and to stay for the wrong reasons. AES, a global independent power producer in Arlington, Virginia, has a relatively short vesting period for retirement-plan contributions and tries not to pay the highest salaries for jobs in its local labor market. By so doing, it seeks to ensure that people are not locked into working at a place where they don't want to be simply for the money.

Managers must also recognize that pay has substantive and symbolic components. In signaling what and who in the organization is valued, pay both reflects and helps determine the organization's culture. Therefore, managers must make sure that the messages sent by pay practices are intended. Talking about teamwork and cooperation and then not having a group-based component to the pay system matters because paying solely on an individual basis signals what the organization believes is actually important—individual behavior and performance. Talking about the importance of all people in the organization and then paying some disproportionately more than others belies that message. One need not go to the extreme of Whole Foods Market, which pays no one more than eight times the average company salary (the result being close to $1 billion in sales at a company where the CEO makes less than $200,000 a year). But paying large executive bonuses while laying off people and asking for wage freezes, as General Motors did in the 1980s, may not send the right message, either. When Southwest Airlines asked its pilots for a five-year wage freeze, CEO Herb Kelleher voluntarily asked the compensation committee to freeze his salary for at least four years as well. The message of shared, common fate is powerful in an organization truly seeking to build a culture of teamwork.

Making pay practices public also sends a powerful symbolic message. Some organizations reveal pay distributions by position or level. A few organizations, such as Whole Foods Market, actually make data on individual pay available to all members who are interested. Other organizations try to maintain a high level of secrecy about pay. What message do those organizations send? Keeping salaries secret suggests that the organization has something to hide or that it doesn't trust its people with the information. Moreover, keeping things secret just encourages people to uncover the secrets—if something is worth hiding, it must be important and interesting enough to expend effort discovering. Pay systems that are more open and transparent send a positive message about the equity of the system and the trust that the company places in its people.

Managers should also consider using other methods besides pay to signal company values and focus behavior. The head of North American sales and operations for the SAS Institute has a useful perspective on this issue. He didn't think he was smart enough to design an incentive system that couldn't be gamed. Instead of using the pay system to signal what was important, he and other SAS managers simply told people what was important for the company and why. That resulted in much more nuanced and rapid changes in behavior because the company didn't have to change the compensation system every time business priorities altered a little. What a novel idea—actually talking to people about what is important and why, rather than trying to send some subtle signals through the compensation system!

Perhaps most important, leaders must come to see pay for what it is: just one element in a set of management practices that can either build or reduce commitment, teamwork, and performance. Thus my final piece of advice about pay is to make sure that pay practices are congruent with other management practices and reinforce rather than oppose their effects.

Breaking with Convention to Break the Myths

Many organizations devote enormous amounts of time and energy to their pay systems, but people, from senior managers to hourly workers, remain unhappy with them. Organizations are trapped in unproductive ways of approaching

Pay cannot substitute for a working environment high on trust, fun, and meaningful work.

pay, which they find difficult to escape. The reason, I would suggest, is that people are afraid to challenge the myths about compensation. It's easier and less contro-versial to see what everyone else is doing and then to do the same. In fact, when I talk to executives at companies about installing pay systems that actually work, I usually hear, "But that's different from what most other compa-nies are saying and doing."

It must certainly be the case that a company cannot earn "abnormal" returns by following the crowd. That's true about marketplace strategies, and it's true about compensation. Companies that are truly exceptional are not trapped by convention but instead see and pursue a better business model.

Companies that have successfully transcended the myths about pay know that pay cannot substitute for a working environment high on trust, fun, and meaningful work. They also know that it is more important to worry about what people do than what they cost, and that zero-sum pay plans can set off internal competition that makes learning from others, teamwork, and cross-func-tional cooperation a dream rather than the way the place works on an everyday basis.

There is an interesting paradox in achieving high organizational performance through innovative pay practices—if it were easy to do, it wouldn't provide as much competitive leverage as it actually does. So while I can review the logic and evidence and offer some alternative ways of thinking about pay, it is the job of leaders to exercise both the judgment and the courage necessary to break with common practice. Those who do will develop organizations in which pay practices actually contribute rather than detract from building high-performance management systems. Those who are stuck in the past are probably doomed to endless tinkering with pay; at the end of the day, they won't have accomplished much, but they will have expended a lot of time and money doing it.

Truth and Consequences: The Six Dangerous Myths About Compensation

Myth	Reality
1. Labor rates and labor costs are the same thing.	1. They are not, and confusing them leads to a host of managerial missteps. For the record, labor rates are straight wages divided by time—a Wal-Mart cashier earns $5.15 an hour, a Wall Street attorney $2,000 a day. Labor costs are a calculation of how much a company pays its people and how much they produce. Thus

German factory workers may be paid at a rate of $30 an hour and Indonesians $3, but the workers' relative costs will reflect how many widgets are produced in the same period of time.

2. You can lower your labor costs by cutting labor rates.

2. When managers buy into the myth that labor rates and labor costs are the same thing, they usually fall for this myth as well. Once again, then, labor costs are a function of labor rates and productivity. To lower labor costs, you need to address *both*. Indeed, sometimes lowering labor rates increases labor costs.

3. Labor costs constitute a significant proportion of total costs.

3. This is true—but only sometimes. Labor costs as a proportion of total costs vary widely by industry and company. Yet many executives assume labor costs are the biggest expense on their income statement. In fact, labor costs are only the most immediately malleable expense.

4. Low labor costs are a potent and sustainable competitive weapon.

4. In fact, labor costs are perhaps the most slippery and least sustainable way to compete. Better to achieve competitive advantage through quality; through customer service; through product, process, or service innovation; or through technology leadership. It is much more difficult to imitate these sources of competitive advantage than to merely cut costs.

5. Individual incentive pay improves performance.

5. Individual incentive pay, in reality, undermines performance—of both the individual and the organization. Many studies strongly suggest that this form of reward undermines teamwork, encourages a short-term focus, and leads people to believe that pay is not related to performance at all but to having the "right" relationships and an ingratiating personality.

6. People work for money.

6. People do work for money—but they work even more for meaning in their lives. In fact, they work to have fun. Companies that ignore this fact are essentially bribing their employees and will pay the price in a lack of loyalty and commitment.

Notes

1. John T. Dunlop and David Weil, "Diffusion and Performance of Modular Production in the U.S. Apparel Industry," *Industrial Relations,* July 1996, p. 337.

2. For the survey of the pay practices of *Fortune* 1,000 companies, see Gerald E. Ledford, Jr., Edward E. Lawler III, and Susan A. Mohrman, "Reward Innovations in *Fortune* 1,000 Companies," *Compensation and Benefits Review,* April 1995, p. 76; for the salary and commission data, see Gregory A. Patterson, "Distressed Shoppers, Disaffected Workers Prompt Stores to Alter Sales Commissions," the *Wall Street Journal,* July 1, 1992, p. B1; for the study of U.K. pay practices, see Stephen Wood, "High Commitment Management and Payment Systems," *Journal of Management Studies,* January 1996, p. 53.

3. For the Social Security Administration study, see Jone L. Pearce, William B. Stevenson, and James L. Perry, "Managerial Compensation Based on Organizational Performance: A Time Series Analysis of the Effects of Merit Pay," *Academy of Management Journal,* June 1985, p. 261; for the study of group-oriented compensation, see Larry Hatcher and Timothy L. Ross, "From Individual Incentives to an Organization-Wide Gainsharing Plan: Effects on Teamwork and Product Quality," *Journal of Organizational Behavior,* May 1991, p. 169.

4. Gerald Marwell, "Altruism and the Problem of Collective Action," in V.J. Derlega and J. Grzelak, eds., *Cooperation and Helping Behavior: Theories and Research* (New York Academic Press, 1982), p. 208.

Originally published in May–June 1998
Reprint 98309

Empowerment

The Emperor's New Clothes

CHRIS ARGYRIS

Executive Summary

EVERYONE TALKS ABOUT EMPOWERMENT, but it's not working. CEOs subtly undermine empowerment. Employees are often unprepared or unwilling to assume the new responsibilities it entails. Even change professionals stifle it.

When empowerment is used as the ultimate criteria of success in organizations, it covers up many of the deeper problems that they must overcome. To understand this apparent contradiction, the author explores two kinds of commitment: external and internal.

External commitment—or contractual compliance—is what employees display when they have little control over their destinies and are accustomed to working under the command-and-control model. *Internal commitment* occurs when employees are committed to a particular project, person, or program for their own individual reasons or motivations. Internal commitment is very closely allied with empowerment.

The problem with change programs designed to encourage empowerment is that they actually end up creating more external than internal commitment. One reason is that these programs are rife with inner contradictions and send out mixed messages like "do your own thing—the way we tell you." The result is that employees feel little responsibility for the change program, and people throughout the organization feel less empowered.

What can be done? Companies would do well to recognize potential inconsistencies in their change programs; to understand that empowerment has its limits; to establish working conditions that encourage employees' internal commitment; and to realize that morale and even empowerment are penultimate criteria in organizations. The ultimate goal is performance.

CONSIDERING ITS MUCH TOUTED POTENTIAL, it's no wonder that empowerment receives all the attention it does. Who wouldn't want more highly motivated employees to help scale the twenty-first century? As one CEO has said, "No vision, no strategy can be achieved without able and empowered employees."

Top-level executives accept their responsibilities to try to develop empowered employees. Human resource professionals devise impressive theories of internal motivation. Experts teach change management. Executives themselves launch any number of programs from reengineering to continuous improvement to TQM. But little of it works.[1]

Take reengineering for instance. Although the rhetoric of reengineering is consistent with empowerment, in reality it is anything but that. Both research and practice indicate that the best results of reengineering occur when jobs are rigorously specified and not when individuals are left to define them. Even the GE workout sessions had their greatest success when the problems resolved were relatively routine. Reengineering has led to improvements in performance, but it has not produced the number of highly motivated employees needed to ensure consistently high-performing organizations.

Few executives would deny that there has been little growth in empowerment over the last 30 years. But why that is so remains a riddle. The answer is complex. The change programs and practices we employ are full of inner contradictions that cripple innovation, motivation, and drive. At the same time, CEOs subtly undermine empowerment. Managers love empowerment in theory, but the command-and-control model is what they trust and know best. For their part, employees are often ambivalent about empowerment—it is great as long as they are not held personally accountable. Even the change professionals often stifle empowerment. Thus, despite all the best efforts that have gone into fostering empowerment, it remains very much like the emperor's new clothes: we praise it loudly in public and ask ourselves privately why we can't see it. There has been no transformation in the workforce, and there has been no sweeping metamorphosis.

Two Kinds of Commitment

To understand why there has been no transformation, we need to begin with commitment. Commitment is not simply a human relations concept. It is an idea that is fundamental to our thinking about economics, strategy, financial governance, information technology, and operations. Commitment is about generating human energy and activating the human mind. Without it, the implementation of any new initiative or idea would be seriously compromised. Human beings can commit themselves in two fundamentally different ways: externally and internally. Both are valuable in the workplace, but only internal commitment reinforces empowerment. (See the exhibit "How Commitment Differs.")

External commitment—think of it as contractual compliance—is what an organization gets when workers have little control over their destinies. It is a fundamental truth of human nature and psychology that the less power people have to shape their lives, the less commitment they will have. When, for example, management single-handedly defines work conditions for employees, the employees will almost certainly be externally com-

---

How Commitment Differs

External Commitment	Internal Commitment
Tasks are defined by others.	Individuals define tasks.
The behavior required to perform tasks is defined by others.	Individuals define the behavior required to perform tasks.
Performance goals are defined by management.	Management and individuals jointly define performance goals that are challenging for the individual.
The importance of the goal is defined by others.	Individuals define the importance of the goal.

mitted. That commitment is external because all that is left for employees is to do what is expected of them. The employees will not feel responsible for the way the situation itself is defined. How can they? They did not do the defining.

If management wants employees to take more responsibility for their own destiny, it must encourage the development of *internal commitment.* As the name implies, internal commitment comes largely from within. Individuals are committed to a particular project, person, or program based on their own reasons or motivations. By definition, internal commitment is participatory and very closely allied with empowerment. The more that top management wants internal commitment from its employees, the more it must try to involve employees in defining work objectives, specifying how to achieve them, and setting stretch targets.

We might well ask whether everyone must participate in order for empowerment to exist in an organization. In principle, the answer is "yes"; in reality, there is a "but." It is unrealistic to expect management to allow thousands of employees to participate fully in self-governance. The degree to which internal commitment is plausible in any organization is certainly limited. Moreover, the extent of participation in corporate goals and aspirations will vary with each employee's wishes and intentions.

At SmithKline Beecham, in one of the most far-reaching programs for employee participation that I know of, management used a merger as an opportunity to build empowerment. Throughout the entire organization, more than 400 task forces were created. Yet to this day top management does not believe that internal commitment has been generated throughout the entire company. Their realistic assessment is that not even all the employees on the task forces feel empowered.

To be fair, it is important to remember that empowerment is a goal that organizations approximate but never quite reach. The fact is that it is possible to have various levels of commitment in an organization and still get the job done. Curiously, employees have no trouble understanding the need to keep within bounds. In all my work, I have yet to find employees who make unrealistic demands about empowerment. For top management, then, the essential thing to know is that there are limits to internal commitment. Employees do not understand—in fact, they usually resent—executives preaching internal commitment while continuing to demand external commitment from the rank and file. Indeed, a great source of discontent in organizations is that top-level managers continually risk their credibility by espousing empowerment too glibly.

Clearly, if it is internal commitment that provides the kind of outcomes that CEOs say they want, then they must be realistic and judicious in their demands for it. But the problem goes deeper because the framework that most organizations are now using to transform themselves discourages employees from actually taking responsibility in their jobs.

Change Programs Increase Inner Contradictions

Major change programs are rife with inner contradictions. By this, I mean that even when these programs and policies are implemented correctly, they do not—and cannot—foster the behavior they are meant to inspire. If the inner contradictions are brought to the surface and addressed, they can be dealt with successfully; that is, they will not inhibit the kind of personal commitment that management says it wants. But if the contradictions remain buried and unacknowledged, as they usually do, they become a destructive force. Not only do they stifle the development of empowerment, they also sap the organization's efficiency by breeding frustration and mistrust.

To illustrate, consider the advice that currently represents best practice for implementing and promoting organizational change. That advice breaks the process down into four basic steps:

- Define a *vision.*

- Define a competitive *strategy* consistent with the vision.

- Define organizational *work processes* that, when executed, will implement the strategy.

- Define individual *job requirements* so that employees can carry out the processes effectively.

The underlying pattern of these instructions is consistent with what change researchers and practitioners have learned about effective implementation over the years. Start with a clear framework—a vision—and progressively make it operational so that it will come alive. So that no one will have any doubts about how to align the four parts of the process, management is advised to speak with one voice. This process makes sense. It is rational.

Yet the process is so riddled with inner contradictions that change programs that follow it will only end up creating confusion, particularly at the implementation stage. Given that all the steps have been so precisely described through a set of instructions, the advice actually encourages more external than internal commitment. Clearly, when employees' actions are defined almost exclusively from the outside (as they are in most change programs), the resulting behavior cannot be empowering and liberating. One immediate consequence is that employees react to the change program by quietly distancing themselves from it. Thus the change program is successful in terms of improving performance because it helps reduce mistakes, as in the case of TQM, or because it helps employees embrace best practices. But at the same time, it undermines internal commitment. In short, the advice for implementing change simply does not provide the new source of energy that many executives want.

But the real danger is that change programs end up poisoning the entire corporation with long-lasting mixed messages. Internally committed employees interpret these messages as "do your own thing—the way we tell you." They reluctantly toe the line. Employees who prefer external commitment will also pick up the mixed messages; however, these people will be relieved because they feel protected from having to take any personal responsibility. In this way, the very working habits that executives do not want to see continued in their organizations are strengthened and reinforced. The result is invariably more inner contradictions and more inefficiency and cynicism, all of which get in the way of real change.

CEOs work against empowerment consciously and unconsciously; executives do not always seem to want what they say they need.

CEOs Undermine Empowerment

CEOs work against empowerment both consciously and unconsciously. Surprisingly—at least to outsiders—executives do not always seem to want what they say they need. Consider a few typical remarks that I came across during my research. These remarks—excerpted from a roundtable discussion of executives from world-class companies—indicate very clearly the ambivalence of CEOs toward internal commitment and empowerment. The first CEO noted that with "well-defined processes where the variances are small and the operating limits are well defined," you no longer need the old command-and-control approach. Workers are now empowered, "provided they respect the process," he said. The second CEO agreed that these "processes are liberating," while the third observed that many employees have a tough time understanding what it means for processes to be "reliable, respectable, and in control."

Let us stop a moment and ask ourselves how there can be empowerment when there is neither guesswork nor challenges—when the job requirements are predetermined and the processes are controlled. For employees operating in such a world, the environment is not empowering; it is foolproof. This is not a milieu in which individuals can aspire to self-governance. On the contrary, as long as they buy in and follow the dictates of the processes, the employees in the companies just described will only become more externally motivated.

Employees won't feel internally committed if someone is always controlling them from the top down.

The enthusiastic use of champions in virtually all contemporary change programs sends a similar mixed message from CEOs to employees. Top management is well aware of the dangers of piecemeal implementation and eventual fade-out in major change programs. They strive to overcome those problems by anointing champions. The champions pursue performance objectives with tenacity, managing by decree. They have generous resources available to ensure compliance, and they monitor employees' progress frequently. Altogether, these behaviors reinforce the top-down control features of the external commitment model. The single voice of fervent champions leads employees to feel that management is in control, and it drives out the sense of internal responsibility and personal empowerment. How can employees feel empowered if someone is always "selling" them or controlling them from the top down? Indeed, such champions would not be necessary if employees were internally committed.

The result of all these interventions is disarray. Managers and the change programs they use undermine the empowerment they so desperately want to achieve. Why does this occur? Could it be that today's top-level managers don't truly want empowered employees? In truth, they are probably unsure. At the same time, employees do not hold executives to task for their behavior. Employees have their own mixed feelings about empowerment.

Employees Have Their Doubts

External commitment is a psychological survival mechanism for many employees—it is a form of adaptive behavior that allows individuals to get by in most work environments. How that survival mechanism works is illustrated quite dramatically today in the former East Germany.

When the Berlin Wall came down, a routine way of life for East German workers came to an end. Most workers had learned to survive by complying. For 40 years, most plants were run in accordance with the dictates of central planners. If many East Germans had pushed for greater control over their destinies, their lives might have been endangered. As a result, East German workers over the years learned to define performance as doing the minimum of what was required of them.

After the fall of communism, I participated in many discussions with West German executives who were surprised and baffled by the lack of initiative and aspiration displayed by the East Germans. What those executives failed to understand is how bewildering—indeed, how threatening—it can be for people to take internal commitment seriously, especially those who have lived their entire lives by the rules of external commitment. As I listened to the West German executives who wanted to make East German employees more internally committed, I thought of several cases in the United States and elsewhere where similar problems exist. Again and again in my experience, prolonged external commitment made internal commitment extremely unlikely, because a sense of empowerment is not innate. It is something that must be learned, developed, and honed.

The question, then, is, How do you produce internal commitment? One thing for sure is that the incentive programs executives have used—for instance, higher compensation, better career paths, "employee of the month" recognition awards—simply do not work. On the contrary, in all my years as a change consultant, I have repeatedly witnessed how offering employees the "right" rewards creates dependency rather than empowerment. Inevitably, the power of such methods wears off with use, and all that has been created is more external commitment.

Consider one company with substantial financial woes. In that case, the CEO decided at considerable personal sacrifice to raise his employees' salaries. But his own research later showed that the employees merely considered their raises to be in keeping with their equity in the labor market. Internal commitment had not increased. Employees continued to do only what was asked of them as long as the rewards were increased. They followed the rules, but they did not take any initiative. They did not take risks, nor did they show the sense of personal responsibility that management sought. The CEO was surprised, but I thought that these results were entirely predictable for two reasons. First, pay, like other popular incentive schemes, often advances external commitment while creating a bias against internal commitment. Second, and more fundamental, many employees do not embrace the idea of empowerment with any more gusto than management does. For a lot of people, empowerment is just too much work. Like the workers in East Germany, almost all employees have learned to survive by depending on external commitment.

When it comes to empowerment, executives and employees are engaged in shadowboxing. Management says it wants employees who participate more; employees say they want to be more involved. But it is difficult to know who means what. Is it just a charade? Employees push for greater autonomy; management says the right thing but tries to keep control through information systems, processes, and tools. Employees see vestiges of the old command-and-control model as confirming their worse suspicions—that superiors want unchallenged power. Management just wants to see better numbers.

Thus the battle between autonomy and control rages on, and meanwhile, as companies make the transition into the next century, the potential for real empowerment is squandered.

Change Professionals Inhibit Empowerment

During the past decade, I have had the opportunity to work with more than 300 change experts in different organizations. Such individuals differ in their practices and their effectiveness, of course, but more striking than the differences are the patterns that recur.

Caught in the middle of the battle between autonomy and control, the change professional has a tough assignment. The role of the change professional, whether internal or external, is ostensibly to facilitate organizational change and continuous learning. In their own way, however, the vast majority of change professionals actually inhibit empowerment in organizations.

To understand how that occurs, consider what happens as Tom, a change agent, tries to work with Jack, a line manager. (Both are composite figures typical of those I encountered in my research.) Jack is told by his boss to work with Tom, who is there to "help" Jack empower his organization. The change program begins with a series of meetings and discussions. Tom talks passionately about openness, honesty, and trust as the foundations of empowerment. Many employees leave these meetings feeling hopeful about the direction that the company is taking toward more open communication. A month into the program, however, Tom observes that Jack has fallen back into his old style of management. He decides that he had better confront Jack:

Tom's unspoken thoughts:	What Tom and Jack say:
Toм: *Things aren't going well.*	Toм: So how's everything going?
	Jack: Things are going pretty well. There's a lot of pressure from above, but we're meeting the numbers.
Toм: *Oh great. All Jack cares about is the numbers. Empowerment isn't even on his agenda.*	Toм: Great. Super. But I was also wondering how well we're doing at getting people more commited to their jobs. How empowered do you think they feel?
	Jack: Well, I think we're doing okay. If there are problems, people come to me and we work it out. Sure, some people are never satisfied. But that's just a few people, and we can handle them.
Toм: *Just what I feared. Jack's not "walking the talk." He just doesn't get it at all.*	Toм: Look, Jack, if you solve all their problems, how are we going to empower our employees?
Toм: *This is hopeless! There's got to be an easier way to make a living. I'll never get through to him. I wish I could tell Jack what I think, but I*	

don't want to put him on
the defensive. I've got to
stay cool.

> JACK: Well, to be honest with
> you, Tom, the signal I'm
> getting from above is that
> my job is to produce the
> numbers without, you know,
> upsetting people. To be fair,
> I think I'm doing that.

What's happening here? The change program that
began with great enthusiasm is clearly in deep trouble.
It's a pattern I've observed over and over again. After the
initial excitement passes, reality inevitably settles in. Put
aside the nice rhetoric of empowerment, employees *will*
have problems. They *will* ask their managers for help,
and their managers *will* tell them what to do. That is
how most work gets done and how organizations meet
their numbers. And in many cases, there's absolutely
nothing wrong with this, except that it goes against the
theory of empowerment.

What does Tom do when he observes Jack telling
his employees what to do? Instead of figuring out
whether Jack is doing the right thing in this situation,
change experts like Tom will almost always be dis-
mayed, because the managers aren't walking the talk
of empowerment. Rarely have I seen a change professional help a manager deal effectively with being
caught between a rock and a hard place. Even more
uncommon is a change agent who offers practical advice to the manager about what to do.

Not only is Tom unwilling to acknowledge the real problem Jack is having, but he papers over his own thoughts. He tries to act as if he still believes the program can be successful when, in fact, he has given up hope. Tom himself is guilty of not walking the talk of openness, honesty, and trust.

In my experience, line managers are far more willing to acknowledge the inner contradictions of change programs—at least, in private. They will admit to distancing themselves from the soft stuff—two-way participation, internal commitment, and discontinuous thinking—to focus instead on the numbers.

Empowerment too often enters the realm of political correctness, which means that no one can say what he or she is thinking.

Managers like Jack often conclude—rightly, I'm afraid—that the change agent does not know how to help them. So Jack listens politely as Tom warns him about the dangers of backsliding and exhorts him to be more persistent. And then Jack goes on about his business.

In the end, everyone is frustrated. In theory, empowerment should make it easier for organizations to meet their numbers. But when change programs are imposed without recognizing the limitations of empowerment and when managers and employees are not helped to deal effectively and openly with them, the organization ends up worse off than it was to begin with. Empowerment too often enters the realm of political correctness, which means that no one can say what he or she is thinking: this is just nonsense. In this scenario, if you challenge the change agent, you become an enemy of change.

So instead of feeling more empowered, people throughout the organization feel more trapped and less able to talk openly about what's really going on. Is it any wonder that change programs don't succeed and that they actually undermine the credibility of top management?

What Is to Be Done?

Despite all the rhetoric surrounding transformation and major change programs, the reality is that today's managers have not yet encountered change programs that work. As we have seen, the reasons for that are complex. Although managers share some of the responsibility for undermining internal motivation in their organizations, the change programs that could create high levels of internal commitment and empowerment in corporations do not yet exist. That is why I believe it is time to begin the research and experimentation that is required to find some viable answers. But for now, let me begin with some recommendations that may help executives think more sensibly about empowerment.

- Recognize that every company has both top-down controls and programs that empower people, and that some inconsistencies are inevitable and must simply be managed. When these inner contradictions become apparent, encourage individuals to bring them to the surface; otherwise, a credibility gap will be created that can pollute the organization for many years to come.

- Don't undertake blatantly contradictory programs. For instance, stop creating change programs that are intended to expand internal commitment but are designed in ways that produce external commitment. Make sure that what is being espoused will not contradict what actually happens.

• Understand that empowerment has its limits. Know how much can be created and what can be accomplished. Know that empowerment is not a cure-all. Do not evoke it needlessly. Once it has been created, do not misuse it. Be clear about who has the right to change things. Specify the likely limits of permissible change.

• Realize that external and internal commitment can coexist in organizations but that how they do so is crucial to the ultimate success or failure of empowerment in the organization. For instance, external commitment is all it takes for performance in most routine jobs. Unnecessary attempts to increase empowerment only end up creating downward spirals of cynicism, disillusionment, and inefficiencies. As a first precaution, distinguish between jobs that require internal commitment and those that do not.

• Establish working conditions to increase empowerment in the organization. If you want to help individuals move away from external commitment, encourage them to examine their own behavior. It has been my experience that many employees are willing to become more personally committed if management is really sincere, if the work allows it, and if the rewards reinforce it.

• Calculate factors such as morale, satisfaction, and even commitment into your human relations policies, but do not make them the ultimate criteria. They are penultimate. The ultimate goal is performance. Individuals can be excellent performers and report low morale, yet it is performance and not morale that is paramount. When morale, satisfaction, and sense of empowerment are used as the ultimate criteria for success in organizations, they cover up many of the problems that organizations must overcome in the twenty-first century.

• Help employees understand the choices they make about their own level of commitment. One of the most helpful things we can do in organizations— indeed, in life—is to require that human beings not knowingly kid themselves about their effectiveness.

Finally, remember that empowerment can run contrary to human nature, and be realistic about how to achieve and use it. To paraphrase Abraham Lincoln: You can empower all of the people some of the time and some of the people all of the time, but you can't empower all of the people all of the time. In the last analysis, nobody should expect more than that.

Note

1. For a description of the similarities and differences in employee-involvement, reengineering, and TQM programs, see Susan Alberts Mohrman, J.R. Galbraith, and Edward E. Alwair, *Tomorrow's Organization* (San Francisco: Jossey-Bass, 1998); J. Hendry, "Processing Reengineering and the Dynamic Balance of the Organization,"

European Management Journal, vol. 13, no. 1, pp. 52–57; T. Eccles, "The Deceptive Allure of Empowerment," *Long Range Planning,* vol. 26, no. 6, pp. 13–21; and B.G. Jackson, "Reengineering the Sense of Self: The Managers and the Management Gurus," *Journal of Management Studies,* 1996, vol. 33, no. 5, pp. 571–590.

Originally published in May–June 1998
Reprint 98302

Making Differences Matter

A New Paradigm for Managing Diversity

DAVID A. THOMAS AND

ROBIN J. ELY

Executive Summary

DIVERSITY EFFORTS IN THE WORKPLACE have been undertaken with great goodwill, but, ironically, they often end up fueling tensions. They rarely spur the leaps in organizational effectiveness that are possible. Two paradigms for diversity are responsible, but a new one is showing it can address the problem.

The discrimination-and-fairness paradigm is based on the recognition that discrimination is wrong. Under it, progress is measured by how well the company achieves its recruitment and retention goals. The paradigm idealizes assimilation and color- and gender-blind conformism. The access-and-legitimacy paradigm, on the other hand, celebrates differences. Under it, organizations seek access to a more diverse clientele, matching their demographics to targeted consumers. But that paradigm can leave employees of different identity-group affiliations feeling marginalized or exploited.

121

In companies with the right kind of leadership, a third paradigm is showing that beneficial learning takes place and organizations become more effective in fulfilling their missions if employees are encouraged to tap their differences for creative ideas. If all or most of eight preconditions are in place, the opportunities for growth are almost unlimited.

Leaders in third-paradigm companies are proactive about learning from diversity; they encourage people to make explicit use of cultural experience at work; they fight all forms of dominance and subordination, including those generated by one functional group acting superior to another; and they ensure that the inevitable tensions that come from a genuine effort to make way for diversity are acknowledged and resolved with sensitivity.

Why should companies concern themselves with diversity? Until recently, many managers answered this question with the assertion that discrimination is wrong, both legally and morally. But today managers are voicing a second notion as well. A more diverse workforce, they say, will increase organizational effectiveness. It will lift morale, bring greater access to new segments of the marketplace, and enhance productivity. In short, they claim, diversity will be good for business.

Yet if this is true—and we believe it is—where are the positive impacts of diversity? Numerous and varied initiatives to increase diversity in corporate America have been under way for more than two decades. Rarely, however, have those efforts spurred leaps in organizational effectiveness. Instead, many attempts to increase diversity in the workplace have backfired, sometimes even heightening tensions among employees and hindering a company's performance.

This article offers an explanation for why diversity efforts are not fulfilling their promise and presents a new paradigm for understanding—and leveraging—diversity. It is our belief that there is a distinct way to unleash the powerful benefits of a diverse workforce. Although these benefits include increased profitability, they go beyond financial measures to encompass learning, creativity, flexibility, organizational and individual growth, and the ability of a company to adjust rapidly and successfully to market changes. The desired transformation, however, requires a fundamental change in the attitudes and behaviors of an organization's leadership. And that will come only when senior managers abandon an underlying and flawed assumption about diversity and replace it with a broader understanding.

Most people assume that workplace diversity is about increasing racial, national, gender, or class representation—in other words, recruiting and retaining more people from traditionally underrepresented "identity groups." Taking this commonly held assumption as a starting point, we set out six years ago to investigate its link to organizational effectiveness. We soon found that thinking of diversity simply in terms of identity-group representation inhibited effectiveness. (See "The Research," on page 153.)

The new understanding of diversity involves more than increasing the number of different identity groups on the payroll.

Organizations usually take one of two paths in managing diversity. In the name of equality and fairness, they encourage (and expect) women and people of color to blend in. Or they set them apart in jobs that relate specifically to their backgrounds, assigning them, for example, to areas that require them to interface with clients or customers of the same identity group. African American M.B.A.'s often find themselves marketing products to inner-city communities; Hispanics frequently market to Hispanics or work for Latin American subsidiaries. In those kinds of cases, companies are operating on the assumption that the main virtue identity groups have to offer is a knowledge of their own people. This assumption is limited—and limiting—and detrimental to diversity efforts.

What we suggest here is that diversity goes beyond increasing the number of different identity-group affiliations on the payroll to recognizing that such an effort is merely the first step in managing a diverse workforce for the organization's utmost benefit. Diversity should be understood as *the varied perspectives and approaches to work* that members of different identity groups bring.

Women, Hispanics, Asian Americans, African Americans, Native Americans—these groups and others outside the mainstream of corporate America don't bring with them just their "insider information." They bring different, important, and competitively relevant knowledge and perspectives about how to actually *do work*—how to design processes, reach goals, frame tasks, create effective teams, communicate ideas, and lead. When allowed to, members of these groups can help companies grow and improve by challenging basic assumptions about an organization's functions, strategies, operations, practices, and procedures. And in doing so, they are able to bring more of their whole selves to the workplace and identify more fully with the work they do, setting in motion a virtuous circle. Certainly, individuals can be expected to contribute to a company their firsthand familiarity with niche markets. But only when companies start thinking about diversity more holistically—as providing fresh and meaningful approaches to work—and stop assuming that diversity relates simply to how a person looks or where he or she comes from, will they be able to reap its full rewards.

Two perspectives have guided most diversity initiatives to date: the *discrimination-and-fairness paradigm* and the *access-and-legitimacy paradigm*. But we have identified a new, emerging approach to this complex management issue. This approach, which we call the *learning-and-effectiveness paradigm*, incorporates aspects of the first two paradigms but goes beyond them by concretely connecting diversity to approaches to work. Our goal is to help business leaders see what their own approach to diversity currently is and how it may already have influenced their companies' diversity efforts. Managers can learn to assess whether they need to change their diversity initiatives and, if so, how to accomplish that change.

The following discussion will also cite several examples of how connecting the new definition of diversity to the actual *doing* of work has led some organizations to markedly better performance. The organizations differ in many ways—none are in the same industry, for instance—but they are united by one similarity: Their leaders realize that increasing demographic variation does not in itself increase organizational effectiveness. They realize that it is *how* a company defines diversity— and *what it does* with the experiences of being a diverse organization—that delivers on the promise.

The Discrimination-and-Fairness Paradigm

Using the discrimination-and-fairness paradigm is perhaps thus far the dominant way of understanding diversity. Leaders who look at diversity through this lens usually focus on equal opportunity, fair treatment, recruitment, and compliance with federal Equal Employment Opportunity requirements. The paradigm's underlying logic can be expressed as follows:

> *Prejudice has kept members of certain demographic groups out of organizations such as ours. As a matter of fairness and to comply with federal mandates, we need to work toward restructuring the makeup of our organization to let it more closely reflect that of society. We need managerial processes that ensure that all our employees are treated equally and with respect and that some are not given unfair advantage over others.*

Although it resembles the thinking behind traditional affirmative-action efforts, the discrimination-and-fairness paradigm does go beyond a simple concern with numbers. Companies that operate with this philosophical orientation often institute mentoring and career-development programs specifically for the women and people of color in their ranks and train other employees to respect cultural differences. Under this paradigm, nevertheless, progress in diversity is measured by how well the company achieves its recruitment and retention goals rather than by the degree to which conditions in the company allow employees to draw on their personal assets and perspectives to do their work more effectively. The staff, one might say, gets diversified, but the work does not.

What are some of the common characteristics of companies that have used the discrimination-and-fairness paradigm successfully to increase their demographic diversity? Our research indicates that they are usually run by leaders who value due process and equal treatment of all employees and who have the authority to use top-down directives to enforce initiatives based on those attitudes. Such companies are often bureaucratic in structure, with control processes in place for monitoring, measuring, and rewarding individual performance. And finally, they are often organizations with entrenched, easily observable cultures, in which values like fairness are widespread and deeply inculcated and codes of conduct are clear and unambiguous. (Perhaps the most extreme example of an organization in which all these factors are at work is the United States Army.)

Without doubt, there are benefits to this paradigm: it does tend to increase demographic diversity in an organization, and it often succeeds in promoting fair treatment. But it also has significant limitations. The first of these is that its color-blind, gender-blind ideal is to some degree built on the implicit assumption that "we are all the same" or "we aspire to being all the same." Under this paradigm, it is not desirable for diversification of the workforce to influence the organization's work or culture. The company should operate as if every person were of the same race, gender, and nationality. It is unlikely that leaders who manage diversity under this paradigm will explore how people's differences generate a potential diversity of effective ways of working, leading, viewing the market, managing people, and learning.

Not only does the discrimination-and-fairness paradigm insist that everyone is the same, but, with its emphasis on equal treatment, it puts pressure on employees to make sure that important differences among them do not count. Genuine disagreements about work definition, therefore, are sometimes wrongly interpreted through this paradigm's fairness-unfairness lens—especially when honest disagreements are accompanied by tense debate. A female employee who insists, for example, that a company's advertising strategy is not appropriate for all ethnic segments in the marketplace might feel she is violating the code of assimilation upon which the paradigm is built. Moreover, if she were then to defend her opinion by citing, let us say, her personal knowledge of the ethnic group the company wanted to reach, she might risk being perceived as importing inappropriate attitudes into an organization that prides itself on being blind to cultural differences.

Workplace paradigms channel organizational thinking in powerful ways. By limiting the ability of employees to acknowledge openly their work-related but culturally based differences, the paradigm actually undermines the organization's capacity to learn about and improve its own strategies, processes, and practices. And it also keeps people from identifying strongly and personally with their work—a critical source of motivation and self-regulation in any business environment.

As an illustration of the paradigm's weaknesses, consider the case of Iversen Dunham, an international consulting firm that focuses on foreign and domestic economic-development policy. (Like all the examples in this article, the company is real, but its name is disguised.) Not long ago, the firm's managers asked us to help them understand why race relations had become a divisive issue precisely at a time when Iversen was receiving accolades for its diversity efforts. Indeed, other organizations had even begun to use the firm to benchmark their own diversity programs.

Iversen's diversity efforts had begun in the early 1970s, when senior managers decided to pursue greater racial and gender diversity in the firm's higher ranks. (The firm's leaders were strongly committed to the cause of social justice.) Women and people of color were hired and charted on career paths toward becoming project leaders. High performers among those who had left the firm were persuaded to return in senior roles. By 1989, about 50% of Iversen's project leaders and professionals were women, and 30% were people of color. The 13-member management committee, once exclusively white and male, included five women and four people of color. Additionally, Iversen had developed a strong contingent of foreign nationals.

It was at about this time, however, that tensions began to surface. Senior managers found it hard to believe that, after all the effort to create a fair and mutually respectful work community, some staff members could still be claiming that Iversen had racial discrimination problems. The management invited us to study the firm and deliver an outsider's assessment of its problem.

We had been inside the firm for only a short time when it became clear that Iversen's leaders viewed the dynamics of diversity through the lens of the discrimination-and-fairness paradigm. But where they saw racial discord, we discerned clashing approaches to the actual work of consulting. Why? Our research showed that tensions were strongest among midlevel project leaders. Surveys and interviews indicated that white project leaders welcomed demographic diversity as a general sign of progress but that they also thought the new employees were somehow changing the company, pulling it away from its original culture and its mission. Common criticisms were that African American and Hispanic staff made problems too complex by linking issues the organization had traditionally regarded as unrelated and that they brought on projects that seemed to require greater cultural sensitivity. White male project leaders also complained that their peers who were women and people of color were undermining one of Iversen's traditional strengths: its hard-core quantitative orientation. For instance, minority project leaders had suggested that Iversen consultants collect information and seek input from others in the client company besides senior managers—that is, from the rank and file and from middle managers. Some had urged Iversen to expand its consulting approach to include the gathering and analysis of qualitative data through interviewing and observation. Indeed, these project leaders had even challenged one of Iversen's long-standing, core assumptions: that the firm's reports were objective. They urged Iversen Dunham to recognize and address the subjective aspect of its analyses; the firm could, for example, include in its reports to clients dissenting Iversen views, if any existed.

For their part, project leaders who were women and people of color felt that they were not accorded the same level of authority to carry out that work as their white male peers. Moreover, they sensed that those peers were skeptical of their opinions, and they resented that doubts were not voiced openly.

Meanwhile, there also was some concern expressed about tension between white managers and nonwhite subordinates, who claimed they were being treated unfairly. But our analysis suggested that the manager-subordinate conflicts were not numerous enough to warrant the attention they were drawing from top management. We believed it was significant that senior managers found it easier to focus on this second type of conflict than on mid-level conflicts about project choice and project definition.

Companies need open and explicit discussion of how differences can be used as sources of individual and organizational effectiveness.

Indeed, Iversen Dunham's focus seemed to be a result of the firm's reliance on its particular diversity paradigm and the emphasis on fairness and equality. It was relatively easy to diagnose problems in light of those concepts and to devise a solution: just get managers to treat their subordinates more fairly.

In contrast, it was difficult to diagnose peer-to-peer tensions in the framework of this model. Such conflicts were about the very nature of Iversen's work, not simply unfair treatment. Yes, they were related to identity-group affiliations, but they were not symptomatic of classic racism. It was Iversen's paradigm that led managers to interpret them as such. Remember, we were asked to assess what was supposed to be a racial discrimination problem. Iversen's discrimination-and-fairness paradigm had created a kind of cognitive blind spot; and, as a result, the company's leadership could not frame the problem accurately or solve it effectively. Instead, the company needed a cultural shift—it needed to grasp what to do with its diversity once it had achieved the numbers. If all Iversen Dunham employees were to contribute to the fullest extent, the company would need a paradigm that would encourage open and explicit discussion of what identity-group differences really mean and how they can be used as sources of individual and organizational effectiveness.

Today, mainly because of senior managers' resistance to such a cultural transformation, Iversen continues to struggle with the tensions arising from the diversity of its workforce.

The Access-and-Legitimacy Paradigm

In the competitive climate of the 1980s and 1990s, a new rhetoric and rationale for managing diversity emerged. If the discrimination-and-fairness paradigm can be said to have idealized assimilation and color-and gender-blind conformism, the access-and-legitimacy paradigm was predicated on the acceptance and celebration of differences. The underlying motivation of the access-and-legitimacy paradigm can be expressed this way:

We are living in an increasingly multicultural country, and new ethnic groups are quickly gaining consumer power. Our company needs a demographically more diverse workforce to help us gain access to these differentiated segments. We need employees with multilingual skills in order to understand and serve our customers better and to gain legitimacy with them. Diversity isn't just fair; it makes business sense.

Where this paradigm has taken hold, organizations have pushed for access to—and legitimacy with—a more diverse clientele by matching the demographics of the organization to those of critical consumer or constituent groups. In some cases, the effort has led to substantial increases in organizational diversity. In investment banks, for example, municipal finance departments have long led corporate finance departments in pursuing demographic diversity because of the typical makeup of the administration of city halls and county boards. Many consumer-products companies that have used market segmentation based on gender, racial, and other demographic differences have also frequently created dedicated marketing positions for each segment. The paradigm has therefore led to new professional and managerial opportunities for women and people of color.

What are the common characteristics of organizations that have successfully used the access-and-legitimacy paradigm to increase their demographic diversity? There is but one: such companies almost always operate in a business environment in which there is increased diversity among customers, clients, or the labor pool—and therefore a clear opportunity or an imminent threat to the company.

Again, the paradigm has its strengths. Its market-based motivation and the potential for competitive advantage that it suggests are often qualities an entire company can understand and therefore support. But the paradigm is perhaps more notable for its limitations. In their pursuit of niche markets, access-and-legitimacy organizations tend to emphasize the role of cultural differences in a company without really analyzing those differences to see how they actually affect the work that is done. Whereas discrimination-and-fairness leaders are too quick to subvert differences in the interest of preserving harmony, access-and-legitimacy leaders are too quick to push staff with niche capabilities into differentiated pigeonholes without trying to understand what those capabilities really are and how they could be integrated into the company's mainstream work. To illustrate our point, we present the case of Access Capital.

Access Capital International is a U.S. investment bank that in the early 1980s launched an aggressive plan to expand into Europe. Initially, however, Access encountered serious problems opening offices in international markets; the people from the United States who were installed abroad lacked credibility, were ignorant of local cultural norms and market conditions, and simply couldn't seem to connect with native clients. Access responded by hiring Europeans who had attended North American business schools and by assigning them in teams to the foreign offices. This strategy was a marked success. Before long, the leaders of Access could take enormous pride in the fact that their European operations were highly profitable and staffed by a truly international corps of professionals. They took to calling the company "the best investment bank in the world."

Several years passed. Access's foreign offices continued to thrive, but some leaders were beginning to sense that the company was not fully benefiting from its diversity efforts. Indeed, some even suspected that the bank had made itself vulnerable because of how it had chosen to manage diversity. A senior executive from the United States explains:

> *If the French team all resigned tomorrow, what would we do? I'm not sure what we could do! We've never attempted to learn what these differences and cultural competencies really are, how they change the process of doing business. What is the German country team actually doing? We don't know. We know they're good, but we don't know the subtleties of how they do what they do. We assumed—and I think correctly—that culture makes a difference, but that's about as far as we went. We hired Europeans with American M.B.A.'s because we didn't know why we couldn't do business in Europe—we just assumed there was something cultural about why we couldn't connect. And ten years later, we still don't know*

*what it is. If we knew, then perhaps we could take it and
teach it. Which part of the investment banking process is
universal and which part of it draws upon particular cultural competencies? What are the commonalities and
differences? I may not be German, but maybe I could do
better at understanding what it means to be an American
doing business in Germany. Our company's biggest failing is that the department heads in London and the directors of the various country teams have never talked
about these cultural identity issues openly. We knew
enough to use people's cultural strengths, as it were, but
we never seemed to learn from them.*

Access's story makes an important point about the
main limitation of the access-and-legitimacy paradigm:
under its influence, the motivation for diversity usually
emerges from very immediate and often crisis-oriented
needs for access and legiti-
macy—in this case, the
need to broker deals in
European markets. How-
ever, once the organiza-
tion appears to be achieving its goal, the leaders
seldom go on to identify

**When a business regards
employees' experience
as useful only to gain
access to narrow markets,
those employees may
feel exploited.**

and analyze the culturally based skills, beliefs, and practices that worked so well. Nor do they consider how the
organization can incorporate and learn from those skills,
beliefs, or practices in order to capitalize on diversity in
the long run.

Under the access-and-legitimacy paradigm, it was as
if the bank's country teams had become little spin-off
companies in their own right, doing their own exotic,
slightly mysterious cultural-diversity thing in a niche

market of their own, using competencies that for some reason could not become more fully integrated into the larger organization's understanding of itself. Difference was valued within Access Capital—hence the development of country teams in the first place—but not valued enough that the organization would try to integrate it into the very core of its culture and into its business practices.

Finally, the access-and-legitimacy paradigm can leave some employees feeling exploited. Many organizations using this paradigm have diversified only in those areas in which they interact with particular niche-market segments. In time, many individuals recruited for this function have come to feel devalued and used as they begin to sense that opportunities in other parts of the organization are closed to them. Often the larger organization regards the experience of these employees as more limited or specialized, even though many of them in fact started their careers in the mainstream market before moving to special markets where their cultural backgrounds were a recognized asset. Also, many of these people say that when companies have needed to downsize or narrow their marketing focus, it is the special departments that are often the first to go. That situation creates tenuous and ultimately untenable career paths for employees in the special departments.

The Emerging Paradigm: Connecting Diversity to Work Perspectives

Recently, in the course of our research, we have encountered a small number of organizations that, having relied initially on one of the above paradigms to guide their diversity efforts, have come to believe that they are not making the most of their own pluralism. These organizations, like Access Capital, recognize that employees frequently make decisions and choices at work that draw upon their cultural background— choices made because of their identity-group affiliations. The companies have also developed an outlook on diversity that enables them to *incorporate* employees' perspectives into the main work of the organization and to enhance work by rethinking primary tasks and redefining markets, products, strategies, missions, business practices, and even cultures. Such companies are using the learning-and-effectiveness paradigm for managing diversity and, by doing so, are tapping diversity's true benefits.

A case in point is Dewey & Levin, a small public-interest law firm located in a northeastern U.S. city. Although Dewey & Levin had long been a profitable practice, by the mid-1980s its all-white legal staff had become concerned that the women they represented in employment-related disputes were exclusively white. The firm's attorneys viewed that fact as a deficiency in light of their mandate to advocate on behalf of all women. Using the thinking behind the access-and-legitimacy paradigm, they also saw it as bad for business.

Shortly thereafter, the firm hired a Hispanic female attorney. The partners' hope, simply put, was that she would bring in clients from her own community and also demonstrate the firm's commitment to representing all women. But something even bigger than that happened. The new attorney introduced ideas to Dewey & Levin about what kinds of cases it should take on. Senior managers were open to those ideas and pursued them with great success. More women of color were hired, and they, too, brought fresh perspectives. The firm now

pursues cases that its previously all-white legal staff
would not have thought relevant or appropriate because
the link between the firm's mission and the employment
issues involved in the cases would not have been obvious
to them. For example, the firm has pursued precedent-
setting litigation that challenges English-only policies—
an area that it once would have ignored because such
policies did not fall under the purview of traditional
affirmative-action work. Yet it now sees a link between
English-only policies and employment issues for a large
group of women—primarily recent immigrants—whom
it had previously failed to serve adequately. As one of the
white principals explains, the demographic composition
of Dewey & Levin "has affected the work in terms of
expanding notions of what are [relevant] issues and taking on issues and framing them in creative ways that
would have never been done [with an all-white staff]. It's
really changed the substance—and in that sense
enhanced the quality—of our work."

Dewey & Levin's increased business success has reinforced its commitment to diversity. In addition, people
of color at the firm uniformly report feeling respected,
not simply "brought along as window dressing." Many of
the new attorneys say their perspectives are heard with a
kind of openness and interest they have never experienced before in a work setting. Not surprisingly, the firm
has had little difficulty attracting and retaining a competent and diverse professional staff.

If the discrimination-and-fairness paradigm is organized around the theme of assimilation—in which the
aim is to achieve a demographically representative
workforce whose members treat one another exactly the
same—then the access-and-legitimacy paradigm can be
regarded as coalescing around an almost opposite con-

cept: differentiation, in which the objective is to place different people where their demographic characteristics match those of important constituents and markets.

The emerging paradigm, in contrast to both, organizes itself around the overarching theme of integration. Assimilation goes too far in pursuing sameness. Differentiation, as we have shown, overshoots in the other direction. The new model for managing diversity transcends both. Like the fairness paradigm, it promotes equal opportunity for all individuals. And like the access paradigm, it acknowledges cultural differences among people and recognizes the value in those differences. Yet this new model for managing diversity lets the organization internalize differences among employees so that it learns and grows because of them. Indeed, with the model fully in place, members of the organization can say, We are all on the same team, *with* our differences— not *despite* them.

Eight Preconditions for Making the Paradigm Shift

Dewey & Levin may be atypical in its eagerness to open itself up to change and engage in a long-term transformation process. We remain convinced, however, that unless organizations that are currently in the grip of the other two paradigms can revise their view of diversity so as to avoid cognitive blind spots, opportunities will be missed, tensions will most likely be misdiagnosed, and companies will continue to find the potential benefits of diversity elusive.

Hence the question arises: What is it about the law firm of Dewey & Levin and other emerging third-paradigm companies that enables them to make the most of their diversity? Our research suggests that there are eight preconditions that help to position organizations to use identity-group differences in the service of organizational learning, growth, and renewal.

1. **The leadership must understand that a diverse workforce will embody different perspectives and approaches to work, and must truly value variety of opinion and insight.** We know of a financial services company that once assumed that the only successful sales model was one that utilized aggressive, rapid-fire cold calls. (Indeed, its incentive system rewarded salespeople in large part for the number of calls made.) An internal review of the company's diversity initiatives, however, showed that the company's first- and third-most-profitable employees were women who were most likely to use a sales technique based on the slow but sure building of relationships. The company's top management has now made the link between different identity groups and different approaches to how work gets done and has come to see that there is more than one right way to get positive results.

2. **The leadership must recognize both the learning opportunities and the challenges that the expression of different perspectives presents for an organization.** In other words, the second precondition is a leadership that is committed to persevering during the long process of learning and relearning that the new paradigm requires.

3. **The organizational culture must create an expectation of high standards of performance from**

everyone. Such a culture isn't one that expects less from some employees than from others. Some organizations expect women and people of color to underperform—a negative assumption that too often becomes a self-fulfilling prophecy. To move to the third paradigm, a company must believe that all its members can and should contribute fully.

4. **The organizational culture must stimulate personal development.** Such a culture brings out people's full range of useful knowledge and skills—usually through the careful design of jobs that allow people to grow and develop but also through training and education programs.

5. **The organizational culture must encourage openness.** Such a culture instills a high tolerance for debate and supports constructive conflict on work-related matters.

6. **The culture must make workers feel valued.** If this precondition is met, workers feel committed to— and empowered within—the organization and therefore feel comfortable taking the initiative to apply their skills and experiences in new ways to enhance their job performance.

7. **The organization must have a well-articulated and widely understood mission.** Such a mission enables people to be clear about what the company is trying to accomplish. It grounds and guides discussions about work-related changes that staff members might suggest. Being clear about the company's mission helps keep discussions about work differences from degenerating into debates about the validity of

people's perspectives. A clear mission provides a focal point that keeps the discussion centered on accomplishment of goals.

8. **The organization must have a relatively egalitarian, nonbureaucratic structure.** It's important to have a structure that promotes the exchange of ideas and welcomes constructive challenges to the usual way of doing things—from any employee with valuable experience. Forward-thinking leaders in bureaucratic organizations must retain the organization's efficiency-promoting control systems and chains of command while finding ways to reshape the change-resisting mind-set of the classic bureaucratic model. They need to separate the enabling elements of bureaucracy (the ability to get things done) from the disabling elements of bureaucracy (those that create resistance to experimentation).

First Interstate Bank: A Paradigm Shift in Progress

All eight preconditions do not have to be in place in order to begin a shift from the first or second diversity orientations toward the learning-and-effectiveness paradigm. But most should be. First Interstate Bank, a midsize bank operating in a midwestern city, illustrates this point.

First Interstate, admittedly, is not a typical bank. Its client base is a minority community, and its mission is expressly to serve that base through "the development of a highly talented workforce." The bank is unique in other ways: its leadership welcomes constructive criticism; its structure is relatively egalitarian and nonbureaucratic; and its culture is open-minded. Nevertheless, First Interstate had long enforced a policy that loan officers had to hold college degrees. Those without were hired only for support-staff jobs and were never promoted beyond or outside support functions.

Two years ago, however, the support staff began to challenge the policy. Many of them had been with First Interstate for many years and, with the company's active support, had improved their skills through training. Others had expanded their skills on the job, again with the bank's encouragement, learning to run credit checks, prepare presentations for clients, and even calculate the algorithms necessary for many loan decisions. As a result, some people on the support staff were doing many of the same tasks as loan officers. Why, then, they wondered, couldn't they receive commensurate rewards in title and compensation?

This questioning led to a series of contentious meetings between the support staff and the bank's senior managers. It soon became clear that the problem called for managing diversity—diversity based not on race or gender but on class. The support personnel were uniformly from lower socioeconomic communities than were the college-educated loan officers. Regardless, the principle was the same as for race- or gender-based diversity problems. The support staff had different ideas about how the work of the bank should be done. They argued that those among them with the requisite skills should be allowed to rise through the ranks to professional positions, and they believed their ideas were not being heard or accepted.

Their beliefs challenged assumptions that the company's leadership had long held about which employees should have the authority to deal with customers and about how much responsibility administrative employees should ultimately receive. In order to take up this challenge, the bank would have to be open to exploring the requirements that a new perspective would impose on it. It would need to consider the possibility of mapping out an educational and career path for people without degrees—a path that could put such workers on the road to becoming loan officers. In other words, the leadership would have to transform itself willingly and embrace fluidity in policies that in times past had been clearly stated and unquestioningly held.

Today the bank's leadership is undergoing just such a transformation. The going, however, is far from easy. The bank's senior managers now must look beyond the tensions and acrimony sparked by the debate over differing work perspectives and consider the bank's new direction an important learning and growth opportunity.

Shift Complete: Third-Paradigm Companies in Action

First Interstate is a shift in progress; but, in addition to Dewey & Levin, there are several organizations we know of for which the shift is complete. In these cases, company leaders have played a critical role as facilitators and tone setters. We have observed in particular that in organizations that have adopted the new perspective, leaders and managers—and, following in their tracks, employees in general—are taking four kinds of action.

They are making the mental connection. First, in organizations that have adopted the new perspective, the leaders are actively seeking opportunities to explore how identity-group differences affect relationships among workers and affect the way work gets done. They are investing considerable time and energy in understanding how identity-group memberships take on social meanings in the organization and how those meanings manifest themselves in the way work is defined, assigned, and accomplished. When there is no proactive search to understand, then learning from diversity, if it happens at all, can occur only reactively— that is, in response to diversity-related crises.

The situation at Iversen Dunham illustrates the missed opportunities resulting from that scenario. Rather than seeing differences in the way project leaders defined and approached their work as an opportunity to gain new insights and develop new approaches to achieving its mission, the firm remained entrenched in its traditional ways, able to arbitrate such differences only by thinking about what was fair and what was racist. With this quite limited view of the role race can play in an organization, discussions about the topic become fraught with fear and defensiveness, and everyone misses out on insights about how race might influence work in positive ways.

A second case, however, illustrates how some leaders using the new paradigm have been able to envision— and make—the connection between cultural diversity and the company's work. A vice president of Mastiff, a large national insurance company, received a complaint from one of the managers in her unit, an African American man. The manager wanted to demote an African American woman he had hired for a leadership position from another Mastiff division just three months before. He told the vice president he was profoundly disappointed with the performance of his new hire.

"I hired her because I was pretty certain she had tremendous leadership skill," he said. "I knew she had a management style that was very open and empowering. I was also sure she'd have a great impact on the rest of the management team. But she hasn't done any of that."

Surprised, the vice president tried to find out from him what he thought the problem was, but she was not getting any answers that she felt really defined or illuminated the root of the problem. Privately, it puzzled her that someone would decide to demote a 15-year veteran of the company—and a minority woman at that—so soon after bringing her to his unit.

The vice president probed further. In the course of the conversation, the manager happened to mention that he knew the new employee from church and was familiar with the way she handled leadership there and in other community settings. In those less formal situations, he had seen her perform as an extremely effective, sensitive, and influential leader.

That is when the vice president made an interpretive leap. "If that's what you know about her," the vice president said to the manager, "then the question for us is, why can't she bring those skills to work here?" The vice president decided to arrange a meeting with all three present to ask this very question directly. In the meeting, the African American woman explained, "I didn't think I would last long if I acted that way here. My personal style of leadership—that particular style—works well if you have the permission to do it fully; then you can just do it and not have to look over your shoulder."

Pointing to the manager who had planned to fire her, she added, "He's right. The style of leadership I use outside this company can definitely be effective. But I've been at Mastiff for 15 years. I know this organization, and I know if I brought that piece of myself—if I became that authentic—I just wouldn't survive here."

What this example illustrates is that the vice president's learning-and-effectiveness paradigm led her to explore and then make the link between cultural diversity and work style. What was occurring, she realized, was a mismatch between the cultural background of the recently promoted woman and the cultural environment of her work setting. It had little to do with private attitudes or feelings, or gender issues, or some inherent lack of leadership ability. The source of the underperformance was that the newly promoted woman had a certain style and the organization's culture did not support her in expressing it comfortably. The vice president's paradigm led her to ask new questions and to seek out new information, but, more important, it also led her to interpret existing information differently.

The two senior managers began to realize that part of the African American woman's inability to see herself as a leader at work was that she had for so long been undervalued in the organization. And, in a sense, she had become used to splitting herself off from who she was in her own community. In the 15 years she had been at Mastiff, she had done her job well as an individual contributor, but she had never received any signals that her bosses wanted her to draw on her cultural competencies in order to lead effectively.

They are legitimating open discussion. Leaders and managers who have adopted the new paradigm are taking the initiative to "green light" open discussion about how identity-group memberships inform and influence an employee's experience and the organization's behavior. They are encouraging people to make *explicit* use of background cultural experience and the pools of knowledge gained outside the organization to inform and enhance their work. Individuals often do use their cultural competencies at work, but in a closeted, almost embarrassed, way. The unfortunate result is that the opportunity for collective and organizational learning and improvement is lost.

The case of a Chinese woman who worked as a chemist at Torinno Food Company illustrates this point. Linda was part of a product development group at Torinno when a problem arose with the flavoring of a new soup. After the group had made a number of scientific attempts to correct the problem, Linda came up with the solution by "setting aside my chemistry and drawing on my understanding of Chinese cooking." She did not, however, share with her colleagues—all of them white males—the real source of her inspiration for the solution for fear that it would set her apart or that they might consider her unprofessional. Overlaid on the cultural issue, of course, was a gender issue (women cooking) as well as a work-family issue (women doing *home* cooking in a chemistry lab). All of these themes had erected unspoken boundaries that Linda knew could be career-damaging for her to cross. After solving the problem, she simply went back to the so-called scientific way of doing things.

Senior managers at Torinno Foods in fact had made a substantial commitment to diversifying the workforce through a program designed to teach employees to value the contributions of all its members. Yet Linda's perceptions indicate that, in the actual day-to-day context of work, the program had failed—and in precisely one of those areas where it would have been important for it to have worked. It had failed to affirm someone's identity-group experiences as a legitimate source of insight into her work. It is likely that this organization will miss future opportunities to take full advantage of the talent of employees such as Linda. When people believe that they must suggest and apply their ideas covertly, the organization also misses opportunities to discuss, debate, refine, and build on those ideas fully. In addition, because individuals like Linda will continue to think that they must hide parts of themselves in order to fit in, they will find it difficult to engage fully not only in their work but also in their workplace relationships. That kind of situation can breed resentment and misunderstanding, fueling tensions that can further obstruct productive work relationships.

Leaders who appreciate differences fight all forms of dominance, including any functional area's presumption of superiority over another.

They actively work against forms of dominance and subordination that inhibit full contribution. Companies in which the third paradigm is emerging have leaders and managers who take responsibility for removing the barriers that block employees from using the full range of their competencies, cultural or otherwise. Racism, homophobia, sexism, and sexual harassment are the most obvious forms of dominance that decrease individual and organizational effectiveness—and third-paradigm leaders have zero tolerance for them. In addition, the leaders are aware that organizations can create their own unique patterns of dominance and subordination based on the presumed superiority and entitlement of some groups over others. It is not uncommon, for instance, to find organizations in which one functional area considers itself better than another. Members of the presumed inferior group frequently describe the organization in the very terms used by those who experience identity-group discrimination. Regardless of the source of the oppression, the result is diminished performance and commitment from employees.

What can leaders do to prevent those kinds of behaviors beyond explicitly forbidding any forms of dominance? They can and should test their own assumptions about the competencies of all members of the workforce because negative assumptions are often unconsciously communicated in powerful—albeit nonverbal—ways. For example, senior managers at Delta Manufacturing had for years allowed productivity and quality at their inner city plants to lag well behind the levels of other plants. When the company's chief executive officer began to question why the problem was never addressed, he came to realize that, in his heart, he had believed that inner-city workers, most of whom were African American or Hispanic, were not capable of doing better than subpar. In the end, the CEO and his senior management team were able to reverse their reasoning and take responsibility for improving the situation. The result was a sharp increase in the performance of the inner-city plants and a message to the entire organization about the capabilities of its entire workforce.

At Mastiff, the insurance company discussed earlier, the vice president and her manager decided to work with the recently promoted African American woman rather than demote her. They realized that their unit was really a pocket inside the larger organization: they did not have to wait for the rest of the organization to make a paradigm shift in order for their particular unit to change. So they met again to think about how to create conditions within their unit that would move the woman toward seeing her leadership position as encompassing all her skills. They assured her that her authentic style of leadership was precisely what they wanted her to bring to the job. They wanted her to be able to use whatever aspects of herself she thought would make her more effective in her work because the whole purpose was to do the job effectively, not to fit some preset traditional formula of how to behave. They let her know that, as a management team, they would try to adjust and change and support her. And they would deal with whatever consequences resulted from her exercising her decision rights in new ways.

Another example of this line of action—working against forms of dominance and subordination to enable full contribution—is the way the CEO of a major chemical company modified the attendance rules for his company's annual strategy conference. In the past, the conference had been attended only by senior executives, a relatively homogeneous group of white men. The company had been working hard on increasing the representation of women and people of color in its ranks, and the CEO could have left it at that. But he reckoned that, unless steps were taken, it would be ten years before the conferences tapped into the insights and perspectives of his newly diverse workforce. So he took the bold step of opening the conference to people from across all levels of the hierarchy, bringing together a diagonal slice of the organization. He also asked the conference organizers to come up with specific interventions, such as small group meetings before the larger session, to ensure that the new attendees would be comfortable enough to enter discussions. The result was that strategy-conference participants heard a much broader, richer, and livelier discussion about future scenarios for the company.

They are making sure that organizational trust stays intact. Few things are faster at killing a shift to a new way of thinking about diversity than feelings of broken trust. Therefore, managers of organizations that are successfully shifting to the learning-and-effectiveness paradigm take one more step: they make sure their organizations remain "safe" places for employees to be themselves. These managers recognize that tensions naturally arise as an organization begins to make room for diversity, starts to experiment with process and product ideas, and learns to reappraise its mission in light of suggestions from newly empowered constituents in the company. But as people put more of themselves out and open up about new feelings and ideas, the dynamics of the learning-and-effectiveness paradigm can produce temporary vulnerabilities. Managers who have helped their organizations make the change successfully have consistently demonstrated their commitment to the process and to all employees by setting a tone of honest discourse, by acknowledging tensions, and by resolving them sensitively and swiftly.

OUR RESEARCH OVER THE PAST SIX YEARS indicates that one cardinal limitation is at the root of companies' inability to attain the expected performance benefits of higher levels of diversity: the leadership's vision of the purpose of a diversified workforce. We have described the two most dominant orientations toward diversity and some of their consequences and limitations, together with a new framework for understanding and managing diversity. The learning-and-effectiveness paradigm we have outlined here is, undoubtedly, still in an emergent phase in those few organizations that embody it. We expect that as more organizations take on the challenge of truly engaging their diversity, new and unforeseen dilemmas will arise. Thus, perhaps more than anything else, a shift toward this paradigm requires a high-level commitment to learning more about the environment, structure, and tasks of one's organization, and giving improvement-generating change greater priority than the security of what is familiar. This is not an easy challenge, but we remain convinced that unless organizations take this step, any diversity initiative will fall short of fulfilling its rich promise.

The Research

This article is based on a three-part research effort that began in 1990. Our subject was diversity; but, more specifically, we sought to understand three management challenges under that heading. First, how do organizations successfully achieve and sustain racial and gender diversity in their executive and middle-management ranks? Second, what is the impact of diversity on an organization's practices, processes, and performance? And, finally, how do leaders influence whether diversity becomes an enhancing or detracting element in the organization?

Over the following six years, we worked particularly closely with three organizations that had attained a high degree of demographic diversity: a small urban law firm, a community bank, and a 200-person consulting firm. In addition, we studied nine other companies in varying stages of diversifying their workforces. The group included two financial-services firms, three *Fortune* 500 manufacturing companies, two midsize high-technology companies, a private foundation, and a university medical center. In each case, we based our analysis on interviews, surveys, archival data, and observation. It is from this work that the third paradigm for managing diversity emerged and with it our belief that old and limiting assumptions about the meaning of diversity must be abandoned before its true potential can be realized as a powerful way to increase organizational effectiveness.

Originally published September–October 1996
Reprint 96510

The Alternative Workplace

Changing Where and How People Work

MAHLON APGAR, IV

Executive Summary

TODAY MANY ORGANIZATIONS, including AT&T and IBM, are pioneering the *alternative workplace*—the combination of nontraditional work practices, settings, and locations that is beginning to supplement traditional offices. This is not a fad. Although estimates vary widely, it is safe to say that some 30 million to 40 million people in the United States are now either telecommuters or home-based workers.

What motivates managers to examine how people spend their time at the office and where else they might do their work? Among the potential benefits for companies are reduced costs, increased productivity, and an edge in vying for and keeping talented employees. They can also capture government incentives and avoid costly sanctions. But at the same time, alternative workplace programs are not for everyone. Indeed, such programs can be difficult to adopt, even for those organizations that seem to be most suited to them. Ingrained behaviors and practical hurdles are hard to overcome. And the challenges of managing both the cultural changes and systems improvements required by an alternative workplace initiative are substantial.

How should senior managers think about alternative workplace programs? What are the criteria for determining whether the alternative workplace is right for a given organization? What are the most common pitfalls in implementing alternative workplace programs? The author provides the answers to these questions in his examination of this new frontier of where and how people work.

On SEPTEMBER 20, 1994, some 32,000 AT&T employees stayed home. They weren't sick or on strike. They were telecommuting. Employees ranging from the CEO to phone operators were part of an experiment that involved 100,000 people. It's purpose? To explore how far a vast organization could go in transforming the workplace by moving the work to the worker instead of the worker to work.

Today AT&T is just one among many organizations pioneering the *alternative workplace* (AW)—the combination of nontraditional work practices, settings, and locations that is beginning to supplement traditional offices. This is not a fad. Although estimates vary widely, some 30 million to 40 million people in the United States are now either telecommuters or home-based workers.

What motivates managers to examine how people spend their time at the office and where else they could work? The most obvious reason is cost reduction. Since 1991, AT&T has freed up some $550 million in cash flow—a 30% improvement—by eliminating offices people don't need, consolidating others, and reducing related overhead costs. Through an AW program called the Mobility Initiative, IBM is saving more than $100 million annually in its North America sales and distribution unit alone.

Another reason is the potential to increase productivity. Employees in the alternative workplace tend to devote less time and energy to typical office routines and more to customers. At IBM, a survey of employees in the Mobility Initiative revealed that 87% believe that their personal productivity and effectiveness on the job have increased significantly.

The alternative workplace also can give companies an edge in vying for—and keeping—talented, highly motivated employees. American Express president and COO Kenneth I. Chenault says that AmEx's AW initiatives help the company retain experienced employees who find the flexibility to work from home especially attractive.

Finally, AW programs are beginning to offer opportunities to capture government incentives and avoid costly sanctions. Many communities are easing zoning rules to enable more residents to establish home offices. In addition, companies are meeting Clean Air Act requirements—and avoiding hefty fines—through regional workplace strategies with extensive AW components. Finally, tax codes may change to enable more employees to deduct home office costs.

The potential benefits are clear. But at the same time, AW programs are not for everyone. Indeed, such programs can be difficult to adopt, even for those organizations most suited to them. Ingrained behaviors and practical hurdles are hard to overcome. And the challenges of managing both the cultural changes and the systems improvements required by an AW initiative are substantial.

How should senior managers think about AW programs? What are the criteria for determining whether the alternative workplace is right for a given organization? What are the most common pitfalls in implementation? The lessons learned by managers who have successfully launched such programs and by those who are struggling to do so suggest that the best place to start is with a clear understanding of the many forms an alternative workplace can take. (See "Myths About the Alternative Workplace," on page 186.)

A Spectrum of Options

Different companies use different variations on the AW theme to tailor new work arrangements to their own needs. To one company, for example, establishing an alternative workplace may mean simply having some workers on different shifts or travel schedules share desks and office space. AT&T determined that for some groups of employees, up to six people could use the same desk and equipment formerly assigned to one. The company now has 14,000 employees in shared-desk arrangements.

Replacing traditional private offices with open-plan space is another option. In such arrangements, a company typically provides team rooms and workstations in open areas. Free-address facilities are a variation on that format. As Jill M. James, director of AT&T's Creative Workplace Solutions initiative, describes them, "You are assigned to one facility, but you can move around and choose a variety of work settings during the day. You don't have to log in or put your name tag on a specific work space. And everyone can find you because your phone, pager, and PC go with you."

Some companies have embraced the concept of "hoteling." As in the other shared-office options, "hotel" work spaces are furnished, equipped, and supported with typical office services. Employees may have mobile cubbies, file cabinets, or lockers for personal storage; and a computer system routes phone calls and E-mail as necessary. But "hotel" work spaces are reserved by the hour, by the day, or by the week instead of being permanently assigned. In addition, a "concierge" may provide employees with travel and logistical support. At its most advanced, "hotel" work space is customized with individuals' personal photos and memorabilia, which are stored electronically, retrieved, and "placed" on occupants' desktops just before they arrive, and then removed as soon as they leave.

Satellite offices are another form of alternative workplace. Such offices break up large, centralized facilities into a network of smaller workplaces that can be located close to customers or to employees' homes. Satellites can save a company up to 50% in real estate costs, diversify the risk of overconcentration in a single location, and broaden the pool of

The U.S. Army's General Reimer rapidly receives on-line advice from officers around the globe.

potential employees. Some are shells—sparsely furnished and equipped with only basic technology; others are fully equipped and serviced. Satellites are generally located in comparatively inexpensive cities and suburban areas. Most often, they have simpler and less costly furnishings and fixtures than their downtown counterparts.

Telecommuting is one of the most commonly recognized forms of alternative workplace. Telecommuting—that is, performing work electronically wherever the worker chooses—generally supplements the traditional workplace rather than replacing it. At IBM, however, telecommuters comprise an entire business unit. And at PeopleSoft, telecommuting is the dominant style of work throughout the entire company.

General Dennis J. Reimer, the U.S. Army's chief of staff, offers compelling insight into what an executive can do from a remote location. Reimer travels with a laptop and routinely communicates by E-mail with 350 general officers and 150 garrison commanders around the world. Using a Web-based network called America's Army On-line, which also includes an intranet chat room similar to those offered through commercial providers, Reimer can raise issues with his officers and receive advice on key decisions, often within hours. "The network allows me to be productive and to maintain a pulse on what is happening whether I'm in Washington or overseas," Reimer says. "It not only saves travel costs but also enables collaborative teamwork across organizational and geographic boundaries around the globe. Gradually, this is changing the culture from one in which 'my information is power' to one in which 'sharing is power.'"

Home offices complete the spectrum of AW options. Companies vary widely in their approaches to home offices. Some simply allow certain employees to work at home at their own discretion and at their own expense. Others—such as AT&T, IBM, and Lucent Technologies—provide laptops, dedicated phone lines, software support, fax-printer units, help lines, and full technical backup at the nearest corporate facility. One major company goes still further by providing employees who work at home with a $1,000 allowance for furnishings and equipment to be used at their discretion.

Most organizations find that a mix of AW options is better than a one-size-fits-all approach. Indeed, the very concept of the alternative workplace means tailoring the program to an organization's specific needs. AT&T's Creative Workplace Solutions strategy, for example, combines three options: shared offices, telecommuting, and virtual offices. These options can accommodate nearly all of AT&T's office-based functions. (See "AT&T's First Shared Office," on page 189.)

Is the Alternative Workplace Right for Your Organization?

The first step toward determining whether any or all of the AW options I've outlined could work for your organization is to answer a few basic questions.

Are you committed to new ways of operating? For example, are you prepared to overhaul performance measures as necessary to align them with the new ways in which employees work? Are you braced for a cultural tailspin as your employees learn new ways of connecting with one another from afar? Are you committed to examining your incentives and rewards policies in light of the different ways in which work may be completed? Consider what Kevin Rirey, an IBM marketing manager, said about performance measurement and rewards in his unit after the Mobility Initiative was put in place: "We've always rewarded for results, but when you are in a traditional office environment and see the effort that people put into a job, it's very difficult not to reward them at least partly for that effort. We don't tend to do that anymore. We focus a lot more on results than on effort. But it's a difficult transition."

Is your organization *informational* rather than *industrial*? This distinction refers to a management philosophy and style rather than to an economic sector or customer base. *Industrial* in this context means that the organization's structure, systems, and management processes are designed for intensive face-to-face interaction and that employees remain rooted to specific workplaces. In such an environment, the potential for AW arrangements is limited.

Informational organizations, by contrast, operate mainly through voice and data communications when it comes to both their employees and their customers. *Informational*, as used here, does not necessarily mean high-tech. But it does mean that managers and employees are moving up the curve toward information-age literacy, which is characterized by flexibility, informality, the ability to change when necessary, respect for personal time and priorities, and a commitment to using technology for improving performance.

Until recently, AT&T and IBM were among the many companies perceived by customers and analysts as industrial organizations; that is, they were seen as tradition bound, formal, bureaucratic, and slow to change. As former AT&T chairman Robert Allen noted on the company's Telecommuting Day in 1994, "Work is where the phone is, and it's logical that we should work like a phone-based organization. When our initiative began, however, AT&T looked like an antiquated company, with fixed schedules, expensive space, and a heavy hierarchy." When the two companies launched their AW programs nearly ten years ago, top-level managers had already begun to reposition their organizations as informational.

Do you have an open culture and proactive managers? A dynamic, nonhierarchical, technologically advanced organization is more likely than a highly structured, command-driven one to implement an AW program successfully. That's why so many newer and smaller companies—particularly those that are heavily involved in the business of information or in electronic commerce—are using AW techniques with great success and with few transition pains. Yet as we've seen, even tradition-conscious organizations can use such techniques to eliminate fixed costs and facilitate performance improvements. The key is whether managers at all levels are open to change.

Richard Karl Goeltz, vice chairman and CFO of American Express, comments, "It's important to have a multifunction team of senior managers promoting and supporting a virtual-office initiative right from the start. We had three departments involved in our effort: HR, technology, and real estate. The individuals on the team must be enthusiastic and not unnecessarily fettered by traditional approaches. And they must be made knowledgeable about all the key issues—from the ways in which corporate policies may be redefined to deal with various types of problems and opportunities to the different options for providing furniture or allowances to employees. Still, I would be skeptical about whether management by fiat would work very well. It's better to be able to say, 'Here's an opportunity to enable you to do your job better, more efficiently, and more economically. You don't have to use it, but it's here.' What I've seen happen elsewhere—and we're beginning to see it in our own initiatives—is that once a fairly large department takes the first step, others are quick to follow."

Can you establish clear links between staff, functions, and time? AW programs assume that certain jobs either do not depend on specific locations and types of facilities or depend on them only part of the time. To analyze whether an AW program can work in your company, you must understand in detail the parameters of each job you are considering for the program. What function does the job serve? Is the work performed over the phone? In person? Via computer? All of the above? How much time does the employee need to spend in direct contact with other employees, customers, and business contacts? Is the location of the office critical to performance? Does it matter whether the job is 9 to 5? Is it important for others to be able to reach the employee immediately?

Managers who assume that the alternative workplace suits only road warriors on the sales force may be in for a surprise.

If a critical mass of corporate functions cannot work in an AW environment, the potential benefits may be too marginal relative to the required investment and effort. But managers who assume intuitively that an AW initiative is limited only to road warriors on the sales force may be surprised; often, more jobs are suited to a different way of working than at first seems possible. Executives at Dun and Bradstreet, for example, initially thought that only 5% of their global workforce could be involved in an AW program but learned that two-fifths of the company's functions—involving half their employees—could adapt with only minor adjustments in work practices.

Are you prepared for some "push back"? As Lorraine Fenton, vice president of information technology for IBM North America observes, most "twenty-somethings" entering the workforce have never had a private office, so to begin their work life without one is not a traumatic change. But for many employees, the transition from conventional to alternative workplaces is not as easy. Employees who are accustomed to a structured office environment may find it hard to adjust to a largely self-directed schedule, and those who are used to working within earshot of many colleagues may be lonely in a remote setting. Moreover, middle managers, who lose their visual and verbal proximity to their direct reports, have to change the way in which they relate to those employees. In fact, middle managers usually put up the strongest resistance to the alternative workplace, in large part because they feel as though the very foundations of their roles are being pulled out from under them.

Can you overcome the external barriers to an AW program? Even if the work is suited to an AW format and managers and employees alike are amenable to change, physical and logistical barriers may exist. If space is at a premium in employees' homes—for example, if many employees live in small apartments—then an AW initiative that calls for people to work at home may not be feasible. This is a key consideration in U.S. cities and in most countries abroad. In Japan, for instance, there simply is no "swing" space in most employees' homes that could be used as office space; to accommodate a home-office initiative there, employees would have to sacrifice living space. Conducting employee focus groups at the exploratory and planning stages of an AW initiative can uncover such concerns effectively.

Will you invest in the tools, training, and techniques that make AW initiatives work? To improve the chances of an AW program's success, all who are involved must be armed with a full set of tools; relevant training; and appropriate, flexible administrative support. Are you committed, for example, to providing standardized computer software for people working in all locations? Accessible, qualified technical assistance? Do you have the financial resources to provide the above?

Too many AW programs are undertaken with only partial support from the organization. Confusion and frustration inevitably ensue, not to mention drops in productivity. These programs are only marginally successful and might ultimately fail. When an employee at home can't communicate with other employees or clients, access the right information, or easily reach a help desk to solve a technology problem, the initiative is destined to fail. As AT&T's James puts it, "The technology has to work from the start. When you're asking people to give up their space and all that goes with it, you owe it to them to make sure that the systems are flawless. Because employees are mobile, the tools they use are their lifeline. They can't survive without them."

If you have answered "yes" to the foregoing questions, you could seriously consider an AW program. The next step is to drill down into the economics of AW initiatives.

Tangible and Intangible Economics

As I suggested earlier, the main reason for AW programs is to reduce current costs and avoid future ones. For established organizations that are pressed for cash, the savings from relinquishing space and making better use of what remains can dwarf the necessary investment in equipment and training. For young organizations, an AW program can give managers a viable alternative to expensive, long-term lease commitments.

But for the typical enterprise, the economics of the alternative workplace are more complex, and the decision to adopt an AW program rests as much—or more— on intangibles as it does on simple financials. Jerome T. Roath, IBM's manager of infrastructure expense, says, "The obvious savings from real-estate cost reduction may hide qualitative improvements in employee satisfaction and customer service that are less measurable but no less important and in the end might justify an [AW] program."

On the flip side, AmEx's Goeltz comments on how a business might think about satellite locations: "Instead of 2,000 people concentrated in one place, one could consider 100 sites of 20 people each around the country. That might cut real estate costs tremendously. But there would be other critical issues to address. For example, would the company provide cafeteria and health club facilities or instead provide allowances to help people pay for their own? And how does one coordinate HR activities across a dispersed group?"

Managers should look at the economics of a potential AW program from three perspectives—the company's, the employee's, and the customer's—and weigh the tangible and intangible costs against the respective benefits. Tangible setup costs for the company include hardware, software, training, and any equipment or furniture the company provides; ongoing costs include allowances, phone charges, and technical support. In home offices, employees provide their own space and some, if not all, of the furnishings and equipment. Intangible costs for the company and its employees include the time spent learning new work habits and ways of communicating with colleagues and customers.

The act of removing the walls that separate people in traditional offices can foster teamwork.

Aside from real estate savings, the organization benefits from increased employee productivity, recruiting, and retention—usually because AW employees have both more professional and more personal time. In one AT&T unit, for example, the average AW participant gained almost five weeks per year by eliminating a 50-minute daily commute. Employees in home offices and other remote locations also can be more efficient during the workday because they have fewer distractions and less downtime. As AT&T's James notes, "When I have 30 minutes between meetings, I can load in my disk and be productive on the spot." Customer satisfaction also improves: as customers become comfortable communicating with the organization electronically, they can reach employees more quickly and receive more direct, personal attention.

Intangible benefits include closer teamwork and greater flexibility. The simple act of removing the walls that separate people in traditional private offices often fosters teamwork. Stephen M. Brazzell, AT&T's vice president for global real estate, says, "Connectivity between individuals and groups comes in many forms, both physical and electronic. Those in shared offices tell us, 'The new arrangement works. It really helps us communicate quickly and effectively because we're all together.' There is a definite improvement in communication, and communication means productivity." What's more, meetings in the alternative workplace take less time because participants manage their time better; they meet not just to discuss issues but to resolve them.

The U.S. Army's Reimer highlights the importance of intangible benefits in his widely dispersed organization: "The biggest benefit I have found is that leaders who are 'far from the flagpole' in places like Bosnia and Korea have direct access to me and to my latest thoughts on many issues. In turn, I receive feedback from the field army as quickly as I would from my staff at the Pentagon. This empowers our leadership team, and it allows the army to speak and act with one voice on rapidly changing situations."

A crucial intangible benefit of an AW program is the value that employees place on increased personal time and control. Although they tend to work longer hours and may even have difficulty leaving their home offices, AW employees find the promise of flexibility attractive, so they are easier to recruit and retain. As Reimer says, "We are now training soldiers when and where it is needed. This not only reduces costs and improves readiness, but it also reduces the time soldiers spend away from home and family—an ever-increasing burden with our intensive training and operational requirements. This helps us retain quality soldiers and their families."

The chart "AT&T's Creative Workplace Plan" illustrates one company's assessment of its tangible economics. Over the next five years, AT&T's initiative is expected to generate annual savings of nearly $50 million as people become accustomed to and take full advantage of the new style of working. This will be a substantial contribution to AT&T's overall aim of reducing annual occupancy costs by $200 million. The plan begins by defining the ratio of occupants to work space for each type of office, the square feet and cost per person, and the expected savings and payback. Shared-office and virtual-office workers use one-third to one-tenth as much corporate space as they do in traditional offices. Over time, these changes could yield annual savings of $5,000 to $10,000 per person. For a group of 100 employees occupying space that costs $24 per square foot, the savings range from $200,000 to $600,000, and payback ranges from one to three years. AT&T's James, who authored the plan, estimates that some 34,000 employees—one-fourth of the total—could be accommodated in AW settings by 2003.

IBM's experience in the alternative workplace provides another good example of well-balanced cost-benefit ratios. IBM began piloting various AW options in 1989 to reduce real-estate–related costs and to explore the use of technology to support sales. But by 1993, the company's profitability and competitiveness had declined to the point that more fundamental changes in corporate strategy were called for. In that context, the early pilot projects were transformed into a mainstream initiative in the North America sales and service organization—an initiative designed to improve customer responsiveness, reduce costs, and increase productivity.

AT&T's Creative Workplace Plan

AT&T's five-year plan reflects the significant impact of creative workplace initiatives on reducing total occupancy costs. The financial benefits result from five interrelated factors to be implemented over time: shifting from traditional to shared and virtual offices, adopting more efficient individual workspace designs, improving office utilization, reducing total company space, and adjusting the number of occupants using company space. The plan's current benchmarks and overall projections are summarized below.

Benchmarks

			Cost		Savings	
Office Type	Utilization ratio	Square feet per person	$ per person (setup)	$ per person[1] (annual)	$ per unit[2] (annual)	Payback (years)
Traditional	1:1	225	12,000	12,000	NA	NA
Shared	3:1	125	7,500	9,000	450,000	1.4
Virtual	10:1	30	5,000	6,000	600,000	0.8

Projections

	1998				2002				Differences[3]	
Factor	Traditional	Shared	Virtual	Total	Traditional	Shared	Virtual	Total	Total	CWP
Square feet (millions)	28.5	2.8	0.6	31.9	18.3	2.0	0.6	20.9	-11.0	-2.9
Square feet per person	300	200	150	285 (average)	225	125	30	190 (average)	-95	-96
Number of occupants	95,000	14,000	4,000	113,000	81,000	20,000	10,000	111,000	-2,000	+12,000
Annual savings ($ millions)	NA	NA	NA	NA	153	30	19	202	-202	-49

Notes:
1. This metric includes real estate as well as voice and data communications costs.
2. This metric is based on a 100-person unit occupying leased space at $24 per square foot.
3. Differences for each factor reflect the changes in the total portfolio from January 1, 1998 to December 31, 2002. They also reflect the changes attributable to the creative workplace initiative during the same period.

Lee A. Dayton, IBM's vice president for corporate development and real estate, recalls, "Two principles were—and are—at the heart of the initiative. First, we want to reduce our employees' travel time. When they are traveling from one customer to another, or from the IBM office to the customer, they're not productive. Second, if employees are at home or at a customer's office, we want to eliminate the need to travel to an IBM office. And if they're not going to work in an IBM office, we want to eliminate the dedicated space with all of its overhead and services."

Currently, IBM's entire U.S. sales force can operate independent of a traditional workplace. More than 12,500 employees have given up their dedicated work spaces, and another 13,000 are capable of mobile operation. IBM also has implemented mobility initiatives, involving some 15,000 employees in Asia, Europe, and Latin America. Thus, approximately 17% of IBM's total worldwide workforce is sufficiently equipped and trained to work in AW formats, and one-third of all the company's departments have at least some mobile employees.

The results? In 1992, worldwide occupancy and voice-IT expenses (that is, phone-based communication charges) totaled $5.7 billion. By 1997, the total had dropped 42% to $3.3 billion. During that period, real estate savings totaled $1 billion from mobility initiatives alone. Even more telling, worldwide costs per person declined 38% from $15,900 to $9,800, and the combined ratio of occupancy and voice-IT expenses to revenues dropped from 8.8% to 4.2%—a 52% improvement. (See the chart "The Economics of Mobility at IBM North America" for a breakdown of these measures.)

As Roath comments, IBM must keep close watch over voice-IT charges. They are still small compared with occupancy costs and other IT expenses, but they could explode as more people go mobile. Still, Dayton says, "The costs you incur with mobility—IT technology, communications, wireless costs—are all going down, while the relative costs of real estate continue to rise."

Dayton also notes that the key to success is evaluating and managing the initiative with the ultimate business goal in mind: "We cost-justified our program based on reductions in spending, primarily from real estate. From the start, we allowed business managers to make the trade-off between real estate savings and investments in technology. And we insisted on saving more than we spent. Every laptop and cellular phone we bought for the initiative was cost-justified. We also introduced an annual worldwide scorecard that tallied cost and square feet per person. The scorecard applied to manufacturing and development departments as well as to sales and distribution. We published the results internally, and, of course, nobody wanted to be last."

Looking ahead, John Newton, IBM's manager of IT plans and measurements, believes that the company's extraordinary cost savings will plateau: "The main short-term problem in mobility economics is that as more people go mobile, we still need a support structure for them. We are reaching a point of diminishing returns, because we can't keep pulling people out of offices forever. There will be productivity benefits but not occupancy cost savings."

Indeed, any organization adopting an AW initiative can be expected to reach a new plateau—with lower fixed costs, higher productivity, and greater employee and customer satisfaction than it previously experienced. But by redeploying some of the savings into better equipment, technical support, even the company

picnic, the organization that benefits from AW initiatives can realize further dividends in employee commitment and loyalty.

Implementing an AW Initiative

If the economics are favorable, you should consider
implementing an AW initiative. The following guidelines will help you chart your course.

The Economics of Mobility at IBM North America

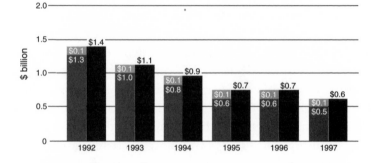

Total Occupancy and Voice-IT Costs

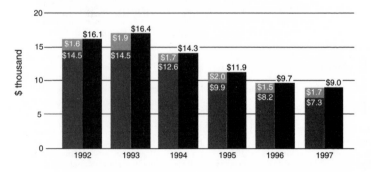

Occupancy and Voice-IT Costs per Person

**Start with a pilot project and don't overcompli-
cate it.** An AW program can be designed either for
pilot testing or for full implementation. The choice
will depend on many factors. If a company is hemor-
rhaging, then a full-scale rollout makes sense: the need
for radical change to reduce costs will be clearly and
universally understood. And if the company already is
informational, with a large number of travelers and
independent workers, then the risk of failing at full

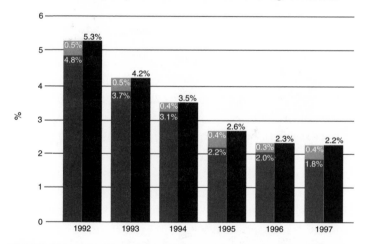

Occupancy and Voice-IT Costs as a Percentage of Revenue

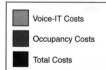

Voice-IT Costs	
Occupancy Costs	
Total Costs	

IBM's entire U.S. sales force can operate independent of
a traditional office. More than 12,500 employees have
given up their dedicated work spaces, and another 13,000
are capable of mobile operation. Managers monitor the
performance of the company's Mobility Initiative in several
ways, including those illustrated at left and above.

The top left chart shows the total occupancy and voice-IT costs for IBM North America.
The bottom left chart, which breaks down those costs by employee, helps managers
assess whether the Mobility Initiative is using space, information, and communications
efficiently. The chart above, which shows total occupancy and voice-IT costs as a
percentage of IBM North America's revenue, helps managers assess the productivity
and efficiency of the Mobility Initiative.

implementation is low. For most organizations, however, an AW program involves so many innovations

A phased approach to an AW program is essential in order to test what's acceptable.

and departures from deeply held norms that a phased, experimental approach is essential to test what's acceptable and to change what isn't. Because this is not "business as usual," it will take extra management time and attention, talented staff, experienced consultants, and some expense to ensure success.

It's a good idea to begin with obvious functions—such as personal sales, telemarketing, project engineering, and consulting—in which individuals already work with their clients by phone or at the clients' premises. Such employees are largely self-directed and need only their phones and laptops to operate in the alternative workplace. Their input could be decisive in ensuring a successful project. In fact, IBM's Dayton credits much of the success of his company's initiative to the fact that it was a bottom-up effort. "We provided direction from the top about our goals," he explains, "but we went deep into the organization to make the program work. Relatively low-level people helped plan it, and local management implemented it. We encouraged them to experiment. It was a peer-driven effort by and for the people who were going to be affected."

David House, president of Establishment Services Worldwide at American Express, began an alternative workplace initiative in 1993 with a pilot project for 300 sales and account service reps in 85 field offices throughout the United States. (See "How Senior Executives at American Express View the Alternative Workplace," on page 193.) By 1995, only 7 offices were needed, the participants were enthusiastic, and customer satisfaction rates had improved. Based on that sucess, a second pilot project was launched at the New York headquarters—a much tougher challenge. Alan Haber, AmEx's project director, says, "The savings from a virtual-office program are much greater at headquarters than in the field offices because we have so much infrastructure and administrative support here. But there's also more resistance to virtual offices. Many people like to come to this building and don't want to give it up."

In foreign operations, pilot projects can be particularly valuable because they allow a company the freedom to experiment in an environment in which cultural and physical differences can be profound. For example, a proactive approach that works in the United States may be counterproductive or downright destructive abroad. The AW concept can best be nurtured in small-scale situations where the local leadership is enthusiastic, the employees are willing to innovate, and the work environment is conducive to change.

Segment the workforce you are considering for the alternative workplace, and assess the logistics of the proposed new arrangement. Whether you're designing a pilot project or rolling out a full program, the first step is to divide the target employees into three segments that define their ties to the workplace: office bound, travel driven, and independent. Employees are best grouped by position rather than by individual, and jobs should be analyzed in as much detail as the data allow. Figuring out the logistics of how employees will work together when they are no longer rooted to a traditional setting is a more straightforward task if you have a clear idea of what they currently do and how and when they do it. Various AW formats can apply to each segment, so the sharper this analysis, the easier it will be to design an appropriate program. The criteria below are not hard-and-fast definitions but guidelines that each organization should adapt to its own situation.

Office-bound staff members spend nearly all their time in a single, fixed, assigned location, whether they are working alone or as part of a team. Their workplace is typically composed of private offices, workstations or "cubes," and meeting rooms. The more these spaces are clustered, the more team interaction occurs, but the harder it is to ensure individuals' privacy. For office-bound workers, desk sharing may be applied in multi-shift operations where work patterns are predictable. For example, two or three people could be assigned to the same office or workstation during daily shifts in a round-the-clock operation, or up to six people could use the same space on different days of the week.

Travel-driven staff members spend at least half their time visiting sites outside their assigned locations, usually for transactions and projects. In fact, their performance is based largely on their capacity to spend as much time outside the office as possible, either with clients (for those in sales and consulting) or while working on projects (for auditors and engineers). Technology can release these travelers almost entirely from their assigned workplaces because they need face-to-face time with clients and colleagues.

Independent employees can set up anywhere and anytime with a computer, modem, and telephone line. In contrast to the other two segments, these employees do not need to be physically present at specific locations. They do not depend on direct contact with clients or colleagues, so they do not need dedicated, preassigned work spaces. Writers, consultants, and scholars are traditional examples of the independent worker. Today, however, individuals in many functions can work independently even though they are members of large, interdependent enterprises. Such people often favor a home office to avoid interruptions; to be close to their families; and to eliminate the time, expense, and stress of commuting. Independent workers also enjoy the freedom to set up their work space according to their personal tastes—an opportunity not offered in most corporate environments where uniform layouts and standard furnishings are the norm.

Monitoring the performance of people you can't see is not easy. Set clear goals from the outset, or your employees may founder.

Make sure that managers and employees are clear both on performance objectives and on how performance will be measured.   In a traditional office, checking on employees' day-to-day progress and altering the course of their work is a relatively straightforward process. But monitoring the performance of people you can't see is quite different. It is all too easy for an employee to founder for some time without his or her manager's knowledge. Setting clear goals from the outset—and agreeing on a way to monitor progress and measure performance—is critical to the success of any AW venture. As Karen Sansone, director of alternative workplace solutions for Lucent Technologies, puts it, "You must get down to basics. Is there a deliverable? How do you know whether the employee or department has done something of value? For some types of employees, performance is clearly measurable. For others, it isn't. While considering different groups for remote work, managers realize that they need both to improve their understanding of what their people are doing and to focus on productivity. Remote work forces managers to think hard about the purpose and results of each job."

Once objectives and measures are in place, the management challenge becomes adapting to a new style of working. Sansone continues, "Remote management is really about a different form of communication. For example, if an employee in a traditional workplace is having difficulty achieving an objective, he or she could pop into the manager's office and say 'I have a problem. I need your help.' Or as a manager, you'd be checking in with them anyway. In a virtual office, people learn different methods. In conventional offices, employees sometimes wait at the door to catch their supervisors for a quick meeting. That's a waste of time you don't come across in the virtual office. What's more, the virtual-office manager and employee set agendas for their conversations so that both are better prepared."

Sansone and other managers agree that some direct contact is essential in the alternative workplace. "Performance evaluation and salary reviews must be done face to face," says Sansone. "So much of the managers' impact comes from sensitivity to individual reactions and the ability to gauge body language as well as words—reactions that simply are impossible to interpret over the phone or through E-mail."

Managers in an AW environment, particularly one in which employees work from a distance, must also pay close attention to time management. When employees are in the office only once a week or several times a month, it is critical that their time is not wasted. In a conventional office, changing the time or the day of a meeting at the last minute may be inconvenient for employees; in a virtual office, it may disrupt their work plans for the entire day, or worse.

Equally important are the peer relationships—so critical to any career—that flourish automatically in the conventional office but could atrophy in the alternative workplace. Joel W. Ratekin, a director of the virtual-office program at American Express, describes the employee's dilemma: "It's a natural response for a manager to grab anyone who is sitting around the office to put out a fire. The remote worker may be even more effective because he may be more focused and might be able to devote more hours to the problem. But for that person to lead or be part of the team, the manager has to think of contacting him." One AmEx unit uses a buddy system in which remote workers have on-site colleagues with whom they must talk every morning. What the employees talk about is up to them. The idea is to keep the remote worker in the loop by encouraging informal chats about new customers, product ideas, job transitions, office policies—the very topics that engage people around the water cooler in a conventional office.

Train for culture as well as technique. So much is new and different about the alternative workplace that managers must reeducate people about what used to be intuitive aspects of office life: when they should work, how often they should communicate, whether to talk or type, and what to say when they do. From an early age, we learn how to live in organizations at particular locations. In the alternative workplace, we have to learn to be in and of the organization while not being at it; at the same time, we have to differentiate our work and family lives while we're at home. Savvy leaders understand that organizational culture cannot be taken for granted in

In the alternative workplace, managers and employees have to learn how to be in and of the organization while not being at it.

the alternative workplace because people are not physically together to create it. But in practice, it is not easy to create or maintain an office culture in certain AW formats—for example, when managers and the people they manage rarely meet face to face. Nor is it easy to figure out how much, or how little, a manager should be involved in helping employees balance the boundaries between work and home life.

Merrill Lynch runs a telecommuting lab to acclimate candidates for the alternative workplace before they formally adopt the new style of working. After extensive prescreening, employees spend two weeks at work in a simulated home office. Installed in a large room equipped with workstations in their conventional office building, prospective telecommuters communicate with their managers, customers, and colleagues solely by phone and E-mail. If they don't like this way of working, they can drop out and return to their usual workplace. To date, nearly 400 people have successfully moved from the simulation lab to their own home offices. The lab has proved a viable way to minimize the risks of placing people in the alternative workplace.

All the organizations I've cited have developed extensive training materials and techniques to suit their particular needs and situations. AT&T's James stresses the basics in a "survival training" course: How do I reserve work space? How do I route the phone and pager? How do I access the database? These companies also use rituals to teach new norms to AW participants—particularly those who will be working from home. Lucent's rituals include such simple tasks as writing to-do lists, dressing for work, giving dependents a good-bye kiss when "leaving" for the office at the beginning of the workday, then tidying up the desk, forwarding calls, shutting down the computer, and watching the evening news at the end of the day. These rituals replace traditional office routines such as morning conversations, coffee breaks, even the commute itself. They also create the breaks between home and work that help maintain a balance. Lucent's Sansone, herself a full-time "home officer," believes that such rituals are critically important for telecommuters because they link the traditions of the conventional office to the new realities of the home office.

Similarly, AW employees adapt to "telework" by creating rituals to suit their new schedules. One Lucent office has established a Wednesday morning doughnut club where virtual-office salespeople drop in for chatter and coffee. They used to meet informally at the water cooler to talk about particularly rewarding sales or problems with customers. Now, Sansone says, they think in advance about what they want to share with the group and the kind of feedback they need. AT&T's James has designed a café at one drop-in facility to encourage "casual collisions": those spontaneous encounters that occur where people gather and communicate. "We also have upholstered chairs with fold-down tables that go across your lap so you can work at them," she says. "It's a different environment—like being back in college."

Educate customers and other stakeholders. Don't expect customers, suppliers, and other stakeholders to understand your new work system immediately. Just as employees need time to ramp up, so too do your outside partners. They must be given the information and the time to adjust. So before launching an AW initiative, let customers and other stakeholders know what is going on. Explain how the new way of working may affect their contact with the organization, stress the benefits they stand to gain from the change, and be patient.

David Russell, a client marketing representative for IBM, says that his customers took a bit of time to adjust but notes that now communication is more efficient than ever: "I'm not in the office as much, so it's more difficult to reach me in person right away. Initially, I think customers found that frustrating. But now they realize that I'm never more than a few minutes away from voice mail and that I can return calls fairly quickly. Many of them are in similar situations; so we communicate a lot more by voice mail. And people have learned that if they don't reach me in person, they should leave a very specific message about the nature of their call so that I can start satisfying their needs immediately rather than playing phone tag."

AW employees must draw a firm line between their home and work lives—and be confident that the line is in the right place.

Keep an eye on how participants balance their work lives with their home lives. If one of the key reasons you are implementing an AW program is to attract and retain employees who will add the most value to your organization, then you must ensure that they are capable of handling the balance between their work lives and their personal lives. Doing so requires a good deal of honesty on both sides. In large part, the solution lies in the employee's ability to draw the line between work and home and to be confident that the line is in the right place.

Two questions on IBM's survey of its AW employees are "How well are you balancing your workload and personal life?" and "Does the company foster an environment that allows you to do that?" As Brad Geary, an IBM techline sales specialist, says, "Even if the company fosters such an environment, the real question is, How well are *you* doing? One of my teammates is in San Diego, and at lunchtime, he goes running on the beach. But he feels guilty that he's out enjoying himself during that part of the day. The company can emphasize the message that as long as it's made up for in some other way and you're still meeting your objectives, it's okay. But the employee has to believe it."

Jeffrey Hill, a project manager for IBM Global Employee Research, agrees that the responsibility belongs both to the company and to the individual. Hill lives in Logan, Utah, and telecommutes with internal clients throughout the country. He reports to an executive in New York whom he sees only several times a year. He says, "It's really about a change in mind-set. When I read the write-in comments on employee surveys, those who have been successful in mobility are really glowing about 'coaching my daughter's soccer team at 3:30 in the afternoon' or 'eating breakfast with my family for the first time in 15 years at IBM.' But then there are others who say, 'I'm always at work. I have my electronic leash. I'm never free.'"

What can be done in the corporate culture to help support a healthy balance? "We get a lot of suggestions that we should avoid highlighting Lou Gerstner's habit of bringing suitcases of work home with him every night," Hill jokes. But as he points out, the true solution lies in an ongoing effort by both the employee and the company to offer positive reinforcement continually, until and beyond the point where both sides are comfortable with the new work arrangement.

O RGANIZATIONS TODAY ARE POISED on the edge of a new frontier: the alternative workplace offers a profound opportunity to benefit both the individual and the enterprise. But beyond one frontier lies another—what one might call a *mobility paradox.* IBM's Dayton explains, "We talk about mobility, but the next frontier is lack of mobility. The alternative workplace—and all the technology that enables it—is changing the way people collaborate." Indeed, we are moving from an era in which people seek connections with one another to an era in which people will have to decide when and where to disconnect—both electronically and socially. Organizations that pursue AW initiatives—particularly those with home office arrangements—must be mindful of that paradox. For only those organizations that balance individual and corporate interests will realize the concept's full potential.

Myths About the Alternative Workplace

MANY EXECUTIVES AND EMPLOYEES HOLD FIRM—but false— beliefs about the alternative workplace. These myths may dissuade organizations from exploring the potential benefits of AW initiatives.

The alternative workplace is for everyone.

IT ISN'T. SOME HIGH-TECH ADVOCATES PROMOTE THIS NOTION, but it is clear that many people and functions today simply are not suited to the alternative workplace. The United States is perhaps a generation away from the threshold of broad-based computer literacy and systems integration that will enable the majority of people to be comfortable working outside the traditional office if they choose to do so. Yet leading organizations, such as those cited in this article, have shown that the AW concept applies to a large and growing segment of the workforce. Ironically, in this new paradigm, the youngest are the most skilled, the oldest are the most awestruck, and the middle-aged are the most resistant to the changes in mind-set and rituals that the alternative workplace requires.

An AW program can spearhead the process of organizational change.

IT CAN'T. Although an AW initiative can leverage reengineering and change-management efforts in the traditional workplace, it cannot launch them. Certain basic improvements must be made first—specifically, simplifying the organization, redesigning business processes, broadening access to information, and defining corporate performance measures. Otherwise, the AW initiative will be swamped by the sheer weight of these changes. But once the tide of change has begun to roll, AW employees can become strong advocates for extending the initiative throughout the organization. After all, they are already self-motivated, relatively autonomous, and results oriented. So they have the most to gain and the least to lose from influencing their peers to accept and adapt to AW work.

A company office is the most productive place to work.

NOT NECESSARILY. What few managers realize—but the alternative workplace highlights—is that the atmosphere and norms of the conventional office can distract people from their work. In a study of one well-managed office, these distractions averaged 70 minutes in an eight-hour day. Employees in the alternative workplace are usually more productive than their traditional counterparts because they learn how to juggle priorities and minimize downtime by making phone calls, writing E-mail, clearing accounts, and performing numerous other routine tasks during the short pockets of time between other commitments throughout the day. But AW employees also are hampered by home and office designs. Developers are just beginning to include quiet, private office space and robust electronics in new homes. Similarly, some new office buildings now include efficient "plug-and-play" drop-in space.

AW employees can take care of themselves.

NOT EXACTLY. It is naïve to think that all one needs is a laptop and a cellular phone to be effective in the alternative workplace. Most people need coaching in the basic protocols of AW life. And everyone needs direct access to the systems, gadgets, and technical support that enable remote work. A person's ability to excel in the alternative workplace depends on an array of new skills in communication, navigation, and leadership that takes time to learn and requires proactive, top-down support. Informal but essential social processes that occur spontaneously in the conventional workplace, such as the brown-bag lunch and the weekly happy hour, need to be managed in the alternative workplace.

The alternative workplace undermines teamwork and organizational cohesion.

IN FACT, it can build them—but in an unorthodox manner. Modern theories of teamwork are based on traditional, face-to-face models in which communication, information, and personal chemistry are intertwined in one location most or all of the time. In the alternative workplace, these links are unlocked. Technology empowers everyone—not just managers—wherever they are by enabling immediate communication with teammates and shared access to information. The chemistry within teams also has different elements. Contributions are defined more by content than by cosmetics when the team works electronically: an objective, egalitarian quality that often is missing in the conventional workplace. And relationships are enriched when managers use "face time" to focus on personal concerns rather than on business tasks.

The alternative workplace is really about computers.

IT'S NOT. The impetus for adopting an AW program is rooted in corporate strategy and renewal more than it is in technology. In a farsighted vision of its business, the U.S. Army is rethinking the fundamentals of its traditional workplace through a high-tech "digitized battlefield" supported by a virtual infrastructure of knowledge, training, and logistics. Similarly, in other organizations, the alternative workplace is really about rethinking the basics: What is the real purpose of your workplace? What work is performed? Who does it? How do they add value? What are their most important needs in the workplace? Where, when, and what types of facilities and systems do they require? How best can you provide them?

AT&T's First Shared Office

RICHARD S. MILLER, vice president of global services (GS) at AT&T, leads some 2,000 sales and support professionals serving major corporations and government clients in the eastern United States. His organization generates $4 billion in annual revenues; its expense budget is about $200 million, of which real estate represents 6%.

In December 1996, Miller learned on a television newscast about a competitor's initiative to pursue an AW program. Driven into action, he asked the help of AT&T's global real estate (GRE) organization in developing a new facility. His idea: a shared office that staff members who spend much of their time with customers outside the office would use as needed, without having assigned workstations. The objective: creating an environment in which teamwork would flourish while reducing real estate costs.

The GRE unit, then in the early stages of developing AT&T's Creative Workplace Solutions strategy, had not yet planned the type of facility Miller envisioned. So he and GRE's planning director, Thomas A. Savastano, Jr., formed a team to consider the alternatives. The team rejected several scenarios. One would have refitted a building already occupied by Miller's group, but that would have disrupted existing operations. Instead, the team opted for a three-part plan: redesign vacant AT&T space in Morristown, New Jersey, as a shared office; move 200 employees from five traditional office locations and 25 others from three satellite offices to the new facility; and redeploy the space to be vacated.

The total group included 58 salespeople, 101 technical specialists, and 66 management and support staff. Miller knew that the staff would need full-time space in the new facility. But he estimated that at least 60% of the sales and technical people would be out of the office with customers at any given time and therefore could share work space. At the time, the GS organization was beginning to transform its technical specialists into *virtual resources;* that is, rather than dedicating individuals to specific customers, these individuals would float from one account to another as needed. That change, Miller reflects, eased the transition from a conventional to an alternative workplace.

The new shared office works as follows: Through their laptops, employees log onto a system to reserve a workstation either before they arrive at the building or when they enter the lobby. Once there, they retrieve their own mobile file cabinet and wheel it to their reserved space. The workstations are six feet square and are arranged in pairs with a C-shaped work surface so that two people can work apart privately or slide around to work side by side. The reservation system routes employees' personal phone numbers to their reserved space. As one occupant says of the new arrangement, "I don't know who is going to sit next to me tomorrow, but interacting with different people all the time helps me think about customer issues more productively. I'm always getting a new perspective and new ideas from others' experience."

AT&T has installed three low-tech features in addition to its high-tech systems. A café encourages people to mingle for coffee and conversation about new sales, customer solutions, and office events. Two large chalkboards allow people to leave messages for others; this feature also reduces the paper flow within the office. And three types of enclosed space—phone rooms, "personal harbors," and team rooms—accommodate private meetings and teleconferences.

AT&T's project shows how significant the tangible and intangible results of an AW initiative can be. It cost $2.1 million to develop, including construction, furniture, equipment, and systems. But the investment was well worth the effort, as the accompanying table shows. Annual savings alone amount to more than $460,000, or $2,000 per person. Over five years, the company will avoid nearly $2 million in costs associated with running a traditional office. In addition, individual space was halved, and team-meeting space doubled. Finally, the project has produced closer teamwork, better customer service, and greater employee satisfaction.

Shared Office Metrics in Morristown

	Before	After
Square feet	45,000	27,000
Annual rent	$1.2M	$0.7M
Five-year expense[1]	$6.4M	$4.5M
Five-year after-tax NPV	$1.9M	$1.2M
Annual rent per square foot	$26	$26
Persons	196	225
Square feet per person	230	120
Annual rent per person	$6,100	$3,100
Annual telecom cost per person	$10,600	$11,200
Total project cost[2]	NA	$2.1M
Total project cost per square foot[2]	NA	$79
Total project cost per person[2]	NA	$9,500
Annual savings	NA	$463,500

Notes:
Figures in the table have been rounded.
1. *This metric includes recurring voice and data charges; without recurring costs, "After" is $3.9M.*
2. *This metric includes total construction, furniture, voice and data installation, and training and systems costs.*

How Senior Executives at American Express View the Alternative Workplace

Richard Karl Goeltz is vice chairman and chief financial officer, and David House is president of Establishment Services Worldwide at American Express. Goeltz has overall responsibility for corporate real estate at AmEx and is a sponsor of the company's AW initiatives. When House joined AmEx in 1993, his division launched a virtual-office strategy in its field offices and has recently completed a similar pilot project at its headquarters. Here, the two sum up some of the salient considerations for managers who are assessing the pros and cons of AW initiatives.

On the benefits of an AW program, Goeltz comments:

THE BENEFITS CAN BE REALIZED in terms of customers, employees, and shareholders. In terms of customers, if a company has a sophisticated, highly efficient network for communications and data manipulation—an essential component of a broad-based virtual-office initiative—then its employees should be able to respond more fully and more promptly to customer needs ranging from simple inquiries to more complex product demands. In terms of staff, we've found that we can draw from a broader pool of people because our employees can be in many locations. Through virtual-office programs, we might be able to attract people with proven records of success who can't or won't move to our office sites. If we can say to such qualified people, "We can offer you a stimulating, rewarding, well-compensated position, and you can work at home," then that is good for the company and for the economy. In terms of shareholders, if a company is giving its customers better service and is realizing savings on real estate and so forth, then naturally there are substantial shareholder benefits.

House underscores the potential:

HERE'S AN EXAMPLE of someone the company would have lost had we not been flexible in our work arrangements. A manager in one of our divisions was going to leave the company when her boss asked me if she could take an open position in our Chicago office but live in Michigan. I told him, "If she's the right candidate, she can live anywhere." She now goes to Chicago several times a month. When I talk with her on the phone, I don't know whether she's in Chicago or Michigan. She travels a fair amount of the time anyway, so it really doesn't matter where she lives. This is a quality-of-life issue for the employee. But for the company, it's an issue of finding the best person for the job.

Goeltz continues:

THE QUESTION IS WHETHER or not a virtual-office program dovetails with the kind of business a company does—whether it can serve an operational need or help improve performance. There are particular opportunities in financial services businesses like ours because our business is information. But each case—indeed, each department or division—must be considered separately.

The two managers agree that getting people to adjust to new ways of working is a major hurdle. Goeltz says:

CONSIDER THE MANAGER who is accustomed to walking into a traditional office and seeing 50 people. In the virtual office, midlevel managers relinquish direct, visual employee supervision. The key difference is that in an information industry, productivity is monitored through electronic systems, whether or not the manager is on site. How many calls does an employee handle? How well and how quickly? If a supervisor periodically wants to listen in on a conversation to determine how a customer representative is handling a call, it doesn't make any difference whether that supervisor is in the next office or halfway around the world, barring time zone considerations. You don't have to be physically present to monitor productivity, efficiency, and quality of customer service. But it is extremely difficult to change the mind-set that really wants that presence.

House concurs, noting that the change is equally challenging from the employee's viewpoint:

IT TAKES DISCIPLINE AND CONFIDENCE for people to feel good about this and say, "Look, I'm going to telecommute. I'm going to work at home two or three days a week, and I'm going to come in here for meetings only twice a week." People have the feeling that if they're not in the office—if they're not seen—they'll be overlooked. One of the ways to overcome that is to encourage telecommuting at senior levels of the organization and let the rest of the company see how it works. I really believe that acceptance of the virtual office is mainly a question of leadership—taking a position and showing that it's now part of our culture.

Goeltz stresses the difference between encouragement and force:

IT IS DANGEROUS, at best, for senior management to mandate an AW scenario. What one has to do is to demonstrate the benefits that can be achieved from virtual-office concepts, satellite offices, and other arrangements that

share the same principles. When the benefits are clear—
be they cost reduction, improved customer service, or
reduced commuting times—then people will be more likely
to embrace the new way of working.

**House observes that participants should understand
the advantages and the limitations of the alternative
workplace:**

THE VIRTUAL OFFICE IS NOT, and should not be, an all-or-
nothing scenario. For example, it is far more difficult to
have a brainstorming meeting over the phone, because
you can't have the same give-and-take and you can't
read body language. And yet it is also critical to understand that time spent in the central office—in the presence
of colleagues—is not the same as it used to be. In the virtual office, if employees come to a meeting, it is for a particular purpose. Something has to be accomplished, or
else the time has been wasted. In the traditional office, a
group of people might meet to *discuss* a certain issue. In
the virtual office, when people meet, they should *decide*
the issue. In the virtual office, the old adage "Time is
money" is taken to a new level: time is money, satisfaction, balance, performance, and a host of other things as
well.

Originally published in May–June 1998
Reprint 98301

The Set-Up-to-Fail Syndrome

JEAN-FRANÇOIS MANZONI AND

JEAN-LOUIS BARSOUX

Executive Summary

WHY DO SOME EMPLOYEES PERFORM POORLY?
Most managers would answer that question by ticking
off a list that includes weak skills, insufficient experience,
inability to prioritize assignments, and lack of motivation.
In other words, they would contend that poor performance is the employee's fault. But is it?

Not always, according to the authors. Their research
with hundreds of executives strongly suggests that it is
the bosses themselves—albeit unintentionally—who are
frequently responsible for an employee's subpar
achievement.

According to the authors, bosses and their perceived
weak performers are often caught in a dynamic called
the *set-up-to-fail* syndrome, which tends to play out as follows: A boss begins to worry when a subordinate's performance is not satisfactory. He then takes what seems

197

like the obvious action by increasing the time and attention he focuses on the employee. But rather than improve the subordinate's performance, the increased supervision has the reverse effect. The subordinate, in perceiving the boss's lack of confidence in him, withdraws from his work and from the boss. And the relationship spirals downward.

What is a boss to do? First, he must accept the possibility that his own behavior could be contributing to the problem. Second, he must plan a careful intervention with the subordinate that takes the form of one or several candid conversations meant to untangle the unhealthy dynamics in the relationship. The intervention is never easy, but the time and energy invested in it usually yields a high payback.

W HEN AN EMPLOYEE FAILS—or even just performs poorly—managers typically do not blame themselves. The employee doesn't understand the work, a manager might contend. Or the employee isn't driven to succeed, can't set priorities, or won't take direction. Whatever the reason, the problem is assumed to be the employee's fault—and the employee's responsibility.

But is it? Sometimes, of course, the answer is yes. Some employees are not up to their assigned tasks and never will be, for lack of knowledge, skill, or simple desire. But sometimes—and we would venture to say often—an employee's poor performance can be blamed largely on his boss.

Perhaps "blamed" is too strong a word, but it is directionally correct. In fact, our research strongly suggests that bosses—albeit accidentally and usually with the best intentions—are often complicit in an employee's lack of success. (See "About the Research," on page 225.) How? By creating and reinforcing a dynamic that essentially sets up perceived underperformers to fail. If the Pygmalion effect describes the dynamic in which an individual lives up to great expectations, the set-up-to-fail syndrome explains the opposite. It describes a dynamic in which employees perceived to be mediocre or weak performers live down to the low expectations their managers have for them. The result is that they often end up leaving the organization—either of their own volition or not.

The syndrome usually begins surreptitiously. The initial impetus can be performance related, such as when an employee loses a client, undershoots a target, or misses a deadline. Often, however, the trigger is less specific. An employee is transferred into a division with a lukewarm recommendation from a previous boss. Or perhaps the boss and the employee don't really get along on a personal basis—several studies have indeed shown that compatibility between boss and subordinate, based on similarity of attitudes, values, or social characteristics, can have a significant impact on a boss's impressions. In any case, the syndrome is set in motion when the boss begins to worry that the employee's performance is not up to par.

The boss then takes what seems like the obvious action in light of the subordinate's perceived shortcomings: he increases the time and attention he focuses on the employee. He requires the employee to get approval before making decisions, asks to see more paperwork documenting those decisions, or watches the employee at meetings more closely and critiques his comments more intensely.

These actions are intended to boost performance and prevent the subordinate from making errors. Unfortunately, however, subordinates often interpret the heightened supervision as a lack of trust and confidence. In time, because of low expectations, they come to doubt their own thinking and ability, and they lose the motivation to make autonomous decisions or to take any action at all. The boss, they figure, will just question everything they do—or do it himself anyway.

Ironically, the boss sees the subordinate's withdrawal as proof that the subordinate is indeed a poor performer. The subordinate, after all, isn't contributing his ideas or energy to the organization. So what does the boss do? He increases his pressure and supervision again—watching, questioning, and double-checking everything the subordinate does. Eventually, the subordinate gives up on his dreams of making a meaningful contribution. Boss and subordinate typically settle into a routine that is not really satisfactory but, aside from periodic clashes, is otherwise bearable for them. In the worst-case scenario, the boss's intense intervention and scrutiny end up paralyzing the employee into inaction and consume so much of the boss's time that the employee quits or is fired. (See the exhibit "The Set-Up-to-Fail Syndrome: No Harm Intended—A Relationship Spirals from Bad to Worse.")

Perhaps the most daunting aspect of the set-up-to-fail syndrome is that it is self-fulfilling and self-reinforcing—it is the quintessential vicious circle. The process is self-fulfilling because the boss's actions contribute to the very behavior that is expected from weak performers. It is self-reinforcing because the boss's low expectations, in being fulfilled by his subordinates, trigger more of the same behavior on his part, which in turn triggers more of the same behavior on the part of subordinates. And on and on, unintentionally, the relationship spirals downward.

A case in point is the story of Steve, a manufacturing supervisor for a *Fortune* 100 company. When we first met Steve, he came across as highly motivated, energetic, and enterprising. He was on top of his operation, monitoring problems and addressing them

---

The Set-Up-to-Fail Syndrome

No Harm Intended—A Relationship Spirals from Bad to Worse

1 Before the set-up-to-fail syndrome begins, the boss and the subordinate are typically engaged in a positive, or at least neutral, relationship.

2 The triggering event in the set-up-to-fail syndrome is often minor or surreptitious. The subordinate may miss a deadline, lose a client, or submit a subpar report. In other cases, the syndrome's genesis is the boss, who distances himself from the subordinate for personal or social reasons unrelated to performance.

3 Reacting to the triggering event, the boss increases his supervision of the subordinate, gives more specific instructions, and wrangles longer over courses of action.

4 The subordinate responds by beginning to suspect a lack of confidence and senses he's not part of the boss's in-group anymore. He starts to withdraw emotionally from the boss and from work. He may also fight to change the boss's image of him, reaching too high or running too fast to be effective.

5 The boss interprets this problem-hoarding, overreaching, or tentativeness as signs that the subordinate has poor judgment and weak capabilities. If the subordinate does perform well, the boss does not acknowledge it or considers it a lucky "one off." He limits the subordinate's discretion, withholds social contact, and shows, with increasing openness, his lack of confidence in and frustration with the subordinate.

6 The subordinate feels boxed in and underappreciated. He increasingly withdraws from his boss and from work. He may even resort to ignoring instructions, openly disputing the boss, and occasionally lashing out because of feelings of rejection. In general, he performs his job mechanically and devotes more energy to self-protection. Moreover, he refers all nonroutine decisions to the boss or avoids contact with him.

7 The boss feels increasingly frustrated and is now convinced that the subordinate cannot perform without intense oversight. He makes this known by his words and deeds, further undermining the subordinate's confidence and prompting inaction.

8 When the set-up-to-fail syndrome is in full swing, the boss pressures and controls the subordinate during interactions. Otherwise, he avoids contact and gives the subordinate routine assignments only. For his part, the subordinate shuts down or leaves, either in dismay, frustration, or anger.

quickly. His boss expressed great confidence in him and gave him an excellent performance rating. Because of his high performance, Steve was chosen to lead a new production line considered essential to the plant's future.

In his new job, Steve reported to Jeff, who had just been promoted to a senior management position at the plant. In the first few weeks of the relationship, Jeff periodically asked Steve to write up short analyses of significant quality-control rejections. Although Jeff didn't really explain this to Steve at the time, his request had two major objectives: to generate information that would help both of them learn the new production process, and to help Steve develop the habit of systematically performing root cause analysis of quality-related problems. Also, being new on the job himself, Jeff wanted to show his own boss that he was on top of the operation.

Unaware of Jeff's motives, Steve balked. Why, he wondered, should he submit reports on information he understood and monitored himself? Partly due to lack of time, partly in response to what he considered interference from his boss, Steve invested little energy in the reports. Their tardiness and below-average quality annoyed Jeff, who began to suspect that Steve was not a particularly proactive manager. When he asked for the reports again, he was more forceful. For Steve, this merely confirmed that Jeff did not trust him. He withdrew more and more from interaction with him, meeting his demands with increased passive resistance. Before long, Jeff became convinced that Steve was not effective enough and couldn't handle his job without help. He started to supervise Steve's every move—to Steve's predictable dismay. One year after excitedly taking on the new production line, Steve was so dispirited he was thinking of quitting.

How can managers break the set-up-to-fail syndrome? Before answering that question, let's take a closer look at the dynamics that set the syndrome in motion and keep it going.

Deconstructing the Syndrome

We said earlier that the set-up-to-fail syndrome usually starts surreptitiously—that is, it is a dynamic that usually creeps up on the boss and the subordinate until suddenly both of them realize that the relationship has gone sour. But underlying the syndrome are several assumptions about weaker performers that bosses appear to accept uniformly. Our research shows, in fact, that executives typically compare weaker performers with stronger performers using the following descriptors:

Up to 90% of all bosses treat some subordinates as though they were part of an in-group, while they consign others to an out-group.

- less motivated, less energetic, and less likely to go beyond the call of duty;

- more passive when it comes to taking charge of problems or projects;

- less aggressive about anticipating problems;

- less innovative and less likely to suggest ideas;

- more parochial in their vision and strategic perspective;

- more prone to hoard information and assert their authority, making them poor bosses to their own subordinates.

It is not surprising that on the basis of these assumptions, bosses tend to treat weaker and stronger performers very differently. Indeed, numerous studies have shown that up to 90% of all managers treat some subordinates as though they were members of an in-group, while they consign others to membership in an out-group. Members of the in-group are considered the trusted collaborators and therefore receive more autonomy, feedback, and expressions of confidence from their bosses. The boss-subordinate relationship for this group is one of mutual trust and reciprocal influence. Members of the out-group, on the other hand, are regarded more as hired hands and are managed in a more formal, less personal way, with more emphasis on rules, policies, and authority. (For more on how bosses treat weaker and stronger performers differently, see the chart "In with the In Crowd, Out with the Out.")

Why do managers categorize subordinates into either in-groups or out-groups? For the same reason that we tend to typecast our family, friends, and acquaintances: it makes life easier. Labeling is something we all do, because it allows us to function more efficiently. It saves time by providing rough-and-ready guides for interpreting events and interacting with others. Managers, for instance, use categorical thinking to figure out quickly who should get what tasks. That's the good news.

The downside of categorical thinking is that in organizations it leads to premature closure. Having made up his mind about a subordinate's limited ability and poor motivation, a manager is likely to notice supporting evidence while selectively dismissing contrary evidence. (For example, a manager might interpret a terrific new product idea from an out-group subordinate as a lucky onetime event.) Unfortunately for some subordinates, several studies show that bosses tend to make decisions about in-groups and out-groups even as early as five days into their relationships with employees.

Are bosses aware of this sorting process and of their different approaches to "in" and "out" employees?

In with the In Crowd, Out with the Out

Boss's Behavior Toward Perceived Stronger Performers	Boss's Behavior Toward Perceived Weaker Performers
•Discusses project objectives, with a limited focus on project implementation. Gives subordinate the freedom to choose his own approach to solving problems or reaching goals.	•Is directive when discussing tasks and goals. Focuses on what needs get done as well as how it should get done.
•Treats unfavorable variances, mistakes, or incorrect judgments as learning opportunities.	•Pays close attention to unfavorable variances, mistakes, or incorrect judgments.
•Makes himself available, as in "Let me know if I can help." Initiates casual and personal conversations.	•Makes himself available to subordinate on a need-to-see basis. Bases conversations primarily on work-related topics.
•Is open to subordinate's suggestions and discusses them with interest.	•Pays little interest to subordinate's comments or suggestions about how and why work is done.
•Gives subordinate interesting and challenging stretch assignments. Often allows subordinate to choose his own assignments.	•Reluctantly gives subordinate anything but routine assignments. When handing out assignments, gives subordinate little choice. Monitors subordinate heavily.
•Solicits opinions from subordinate on organizational strategy, execution, policy, and procedures.	•Rarely asks subordinate for input about organizational or work-related matters.
•Often defers to subordinate's opinion in disagreements.	•Usually imposes own views in disagreements.
•Praises subordinate for work well done.	•Emphasizes what the subordinate is doing poorly.

Definitely. In fact, the bosses we have studied, regardless of nationality, company, or personal background, were usually quite conscious of behaving in a more controlling way with perceived weaker performers. Some of them preferred to label this approach as "supportive and helpful." Many of them also acknowledged that—although they tried not to—they tended to become impatient with weaker performers more easily than with stronger performers. By and large, however, managers are aware of the controlling nature of their behavior toward perceived weaker performers. For them, this behavior is not an error in implementation; it is intentional.

> *What bosses do not realize is that their tight controls end up hurting subordinates' performance by undermining their motivation.*

What bosses typically do *not* realize is that their tight controls end up hurting subordinates' performance by undermining their motivation in two ways: first, by depriving subordinates of autonomy on the job and, second, by making them feel undervalued. Tight controls are an indication that the boss assumes the subordinate can't perform well without strict guidelines. When the subordinate senses these low expectations, it can undermine his self-confidence. This is particularly problematic because numerous studies confirm that people perform up or down to the levels their bosses expect from them or, indeed, to the levels they expect from themselves.[1]

Of course, executives often tell us, "Oh, but I'm very careful about this issue of expectations. I exert more control over my underperformers, but I make sure that it does not come across as a lack of trust or confidence in their ability." We believe what these executives tell us.

That is, we believe that they do try hard to disguise their intentions. When we talk to their subordinates, however, we find that these efforts are for the most part futile. In fact, our research shows that most employees can—and do—"read their boss's mind." In particular, they know full well whether they fit into their boss's in-group or out-group. All they have to do is compare how they are treated with how their more highly regarded colleagues are treated.

Just as the boss's assumptions about weaker performers and the right way to manage them explains his complicity in the set-up-to-fail syndrome, the subordinate's assumptions about what the boss is thinking explain his own complicity. The reason? When people perceive disapproval, criticism, or simply a lack of confidence and appreciation, they tend to shut down—a behavioral phenomenon that manifests itself in several ways.

Primarily, shutting down means disconnecting intellectually and emotionally. Subordinates simply stop giving their best. They grow tired of being overruled, and they lose the will to fight for their ideas. As one subordinate put it, "My boss tells me how to execute every detail. Rather than arguing with him, I've ended up wanting to say, 'Come on, just tell me what you want me to do, and I'll go do it.' You become a robot." Another perceived weak performer explained, "When my boss tells me to do something, I just do it mechanically."

Shutting down also involves disengaging personally—essentially reducing contact with the boss. Partly, this disengagement is motivated by the nature of previous exchanges that have tended to be negative in tone. As one subordinate admitted, "I used to initiate much more contact with my boss until the only thing I received was negative feedback; then I started shying away."

Besides the risk of a negative reaction, perceived weaker performers are concerned with not tainting their images further. Following the often-heard aphorism "Better to keep quiet and look like a fool than to open your mouth and prove it," they avoid asking for help for fear of further exposing their limitations. They also tend to volunteer less information—a simple "heads up" from a perceived underperformer can cause the boss to overreact and jump into action when none is required. As one perceived weak performer recalled, "I just wanted to let my boss know about a small matter, only slightly out of the routine, but as soon as I mentioned it, he was all over my case. I should have kept my mouth closed. I do now."

Finally, shutting down can mean becoming defensive. Many perceived underperformers start devoting more energy to self-justification. Anticipating that they will be personally blamed for failures, they seek to find excuses early. They end up spending a lot of time looking in the rearview mirror and less time looking at the road ahead. In some cases—as in the case of Steve, the manufacturing supervisor described earlier—this defensiveness can lead to noncompliance or even systematic opposition to the boss's views. While this idea of a weak subordinate going head to head with his boss may seem irrational, it may reflect what Albert Camus once observed: "When deprived of choice, the only freedom left is the freedom to say no."

The Syndrome Is Costly

There are two obvious costs of the set-up-to-fail syndrome: the emotional cost paid by the subordinate and the organizational cost associated with the company's failure to get the best out of an employee. Yet there are other costs to consider, some of them indirect and long term.

The boss pays for the syndrome in several ways. First, uneasy relationships with perceived low performers often sap the boss's emotional and physical energy. It can be quite a strain to keep up a facade of courtesy and pretend everything is fine when both parties know it is not. In addition, the energy devoted to trying to fix these relationships or improve the subordinate's performance through increased supervision prevents the boss from attending to other activities—which often frustrates or even angers the boss.

> *One strong performer said of his boss's hypercritical behavior toward another employee: "It made us feel like we're expendable."*

Furthermore, the syndrome can take its toll on the boss's reputation, as other employees in the organization observe his behavior toward weaker performers. If the boss's treatment of a subordinate is deemed unfair or unsupportive, observers will be quick to draw their lessons. One outstanding performer commented on his boss's controlling and hypercritical behavior toward another subordinate: "It made us all feel like we're expendable." As organizations increasingly espouse the virtues of learning and empowerment, managers must cultivate their reputations as coaches, as well as get results.

The set-up-to-fail syndrome also has serious consequences for any team. A lack of faith in perceived weaker performers can tempt bosses to overload those whom they consider superior performers; bosses want to entrust critical assignments to those who can be counted on to deliver reliably and quickly and to those who will go beyond the call of duty because of their strong sense of shared fate. As one boss half-jokingly said, "Rule number one: if you want something done, give it to someone who's busy—there's a reason why that person is busy."

An increased workload may help perceived superior performers learn to manage their time better, especially as they start to delegate to their own subordinates more effectively. In many cases, however, these performers simply absorb the greater load and higher stress which, over time, takes a personal toll and decreases the attention they can devote to other dimensions of their jobs, particularly those yielding longer-term benefits. In the worst-case scenario, overburdening strong performers can lead to burnout.

Team spirit can also suffer from the progressive alienation of one or more perceived low performers. Great teams share a sense of enthusiasm and commitment to a common mission. Even when members of the boss's out-group try to keep their pain to themselves, other team members feel the strain. One manager recalled the discomfort experienced by the whole team as they watched their boss grill one of their peers every week. As he explained, "A team is like a functioning organism. If one member is suffering, the whole team feels that pain."

In addition, alienated subordinates often do not keep their suffering to themselves. In the corridors or over lunch, they seek out sympathetic ears to vent their recriminations and complaints, not only wasting their own time but also pulling their colleagues away from productive work. Instead of focusing on the team's mission, valuable time and energy is diverted to the discussion of internal politics and dynamics.

Finally, the set-up-to-fail syndrome has consequences for the subordinates of the perceived weak performers. Consider the weakest kid in the school yard who gets pummeled by a bully. The abused child often goes home and pummels his smaller, weaker siblings. So it is with the people who are in the boss's out-group. When they have to manage their own employees, they frequently replicate the behavior that their bosses show to them. They fail to recognize good results or, more often, supervise their employees excessively.

Breaking Out Is Hard to Do

The set-up-to-fail syndrome is not irreversible. Subordinates can break out of it, but we have found that to be rare. The subordinate must consistently deliver such superior results that the boss is forced to change the employee from out-group to in-group status—a phenomenon made difficult by the context in which these subordinates operate. It is hard for subordinates to impress their bosses when they must work on unchallenging tasks, with no autonomy and limited resources; it is also hard for them to persist and maintain high standards when they receive little encouragement from their bosses.

Furthermore, even if the subordinate achieves better results, it may take some time for them to register with the boss because of his selective observation and recall. Indeed, research shows that bosses tend to attribute the good things that happen to weaker performers to external factors rather than to their efforts and ability (while the opposite is true for perceived high performers: successes tend to be seen as theirs, and failures tend to be attributed to external uncontrollable factors). The subordinate will therefore need to achieve a string of successes in order to have the boss even contemplate revising the initial categorization. Clearly, it takes a special kind of courage, self-confidence, competence, and persistence on the part of the subordinate to break out of the syndrome.

Instead, what often happens is that members of the out-group set excessively ambitious goals for themselves to impress the boss quickly and powerfully—promising to hit a deadline three weeks early, for instance, or attacking six projects at the same time, or simply attempting to handle a large problem without help. Sadly, such superhuman efforts are usually just that. And in setting goals so high that they are bound to fail, the subordinates also come across as having had very poor judgment in the first place.

The set-up-to-fail syndrome is not restricted to incompetent bosses. We have seen it happen to people perceived within their organizations to be excellent bosses. Their mismanagement of some subordinates need not prevent them from achieving success, particularly when they and the perceived superior performers achieve high levels of individual performance. However, those bosses could be even more successful to the team, the organization, and themselves if they could break the syndrome.

Getting It Right

As a general rule, the first step in solving a problem is recognizing that one exists. This observation is especially relevant to the set-up-to-fail syndrome because of its self-fulfilling and self-reinforcing nature. Interrupting the syndrome requires that a manager understand the dynamic and, particularly, that he accept the possibility that his own behavior may be contributing to a subordinate's underperformance. The next step toward cracking the syndrome, however, is more difficult: it requires a carefully planned and structured intervention that takes the form of one (or several) candid conversations meant to bring to the surface and untangle the unhealthy dynamics that define the boss and the subordinate's relationship. The goal of such an intervention is to bring about a sustainable increase in the subordinate's performance while progressively reducing the boss's involvement.

It would be difficult—and indeed, detrimental—to provide a detailed script of what this kind of conversation should sound like. A boss who rigidly plans for this conversation with a subordinate will not be able to engage in real dialogue with him, because real dialogue requires flexibility. As a guiding framework, however, we offer five components that characterize effective interventions. Although they are not strictly sequential steps, all five components should be part of these interventions.

First, the boss must create the right context for the discussion. He must, for instance, select a time and place to conduct the meeting so that it presents as little threat as possible to the subordinate. A neutral location may be more conducive to open dialogue than an office where previous and perhaps unpleasant conversations have taken place. The boss must also use affirming language when asking the subordinate to meet with him. The session should not be billed as "feedback," because such terms may suggest baggage from the past. "Feedback" could also be taken to mean that the conversation will be one-directional, a monologue delivered by the boss to the subordinate. Instead, the intervention should be described as a meeting to discuss the performance of the subordinate, the role of the boss, and the relationship between the subordinate and the boss. The boss might even acknowledge that he feels tension in the relationship and wants to use the conversation as a way to decrease it.

Finally, in setting the context, the boss should tell the perceived weaker performer that he would genuinely like the interaction to be an open dialogue. In particular, he should acknowledge that he may be partially responsible for the situation and that his own behavior toward the subordinate is fair game for discussion.

Second, the boss and the subordinate must use the intervention process to come to an agreement on the symptoms of the problem. Few employees are ineffective in all aspects of their performance. And few—if any—employees desire to do poorly on the job. Therefore, it is critical that the intervention result in a mutual understanding of the specific job responsibilities in which the subordinate is weak. In the case of Steve and Jeff, for instance, an exhaustive sorting of the evidence might have led to an agreement that Steve's underperformance was not universal but instead largely confined to the quality of the reports he submitted (or failed to submit). In another situation, it might be agreed that a purchasing manager was weak when it came to finding off-shore suppliers and to voicing his ideas in meetings. Or a new investment professional and his boss might come to agree that his performance was subpar when it came to timing the sales and purchase of stocks, but they might also agree that his financial analysis of stocks was quite strong. The idea here is that before working to improve performance or reduce tension in a relationship, an agreement must be reached about what areas of performance contribute to the contentiousness.

We used the word "evidence" above in discussing the case of Steve and Jeff. That is because a boss needs to back up his performance assessments with facts and data—that is, if the intervention is to be useful. They cannot be based on feelings—as in Jeff telling Steve, "I just have the feeling you're not putting enough energy into the reports." Instead, Jeff needs to describe what a good report should look like and the ways in which Steve's reports fall short. Likewise, the subordinate must be allowed—indeed, encouraged—to defend his performance, compare it with colleagues' work, and point out areas in which he is strong. After all, just because it is the boss's opinion does not make it a fact.

Third, the boss and the subordinate should arrive at a common understanding of what might be causing the weak performance in certain areas. Once the areas of weak performance have been identified, it is time to unearth the reasons for those weaknesses. Does the subordinate have limited skills in organizing work, managing his time, or working with others? Is he lacking knowledge or capabilities? Do the boss and the subordinate agree on their priorities? Maybe the subordinate has been paying less attention to a particular dimension of his work because he does not realize its importance to the boss. Does the subordinate become less effective under pressure?

As part of the intervention, the boss should bring up the subject of how his own behavior may affect the subordinate's performance.

Does he have lower standards for performance than the boss does?

It is also critical in the intervention that the boss bring up the subject of his own behavior toward the subordinate and how this affects the subordinate's performance. The boss might even try to describe the dynamics of the set-up-to-fail syndrome. "Does my behavior toward you make things worse for you?" he might ask, or, "What am I doing that is leading you to feel that I am putting too much pressure on you?"

This component of the discussion also needs to make explicit the assumptions that the boss and the subordinate have thus far been making about each other's intentions. Many misunderstandings start with untested assumptions. For example, Jeff might have said, "When you did not supply me with the reports I asked for, I came to the conclusion that you were not very proactive." That would have allowed Steve to bring his buried assumptions into the open. "No," he might have answered, "I just reacted negatively because you asked for the reports in writing, which I took as a sign of excessive control."

Fourth, the boss and the subordinate should arrive at an agreement about their performance objectives and on their desire to have the relationship move forward. In medicine, a course of treatment follows the diagnosis of an illness. Things are a bit more complex when repairing organizational dysfunction, since modifying behavior and developing complex skills can be more difficult than taking a few pills. Still, the principle that applies to medicine also applies to business: boss and subordinate must use the intervention to plot a course of treatment regarding the root problems they have jointly identified.

The contract between boss and subordinate should identify the ways they can improve on their skills, knowledge, experience, or personal relationship. It should also include an explicit discussion of how much and what type of future supervision the boss will have. No boss, of course, should suddenly abdicate his involvement; it is legitimate for bosses to monitor subordinates' work, particularly when a subordinate has shown limited abilities in one or more facets of his job. From the subordinate's point of view, however, such involvement by the boss is more likely to be accepted, and possibly even welcomed, if the goal is to help the subordinate develop and improve over time. Most subordinates can accept temporary involvement that is meant to decrease as their performance improves. The problem is intense monitoring that never seems to go away.

Fifth, the boss and the subordinate should agree to communicate more openly in the future. The boss could say, "Next time I do something that communicates low expectations, can you let me know immediately?" And the subordinate might say, or be encouraged to say, "Next time I do something that aggravates you or that you do not understand, can you also let me know right away?" Those simple requests can open the door to a more honest relationship almost instantly.

No Easy Answer

Our research suggests that interventions of this type do not take place very often. Face-to-face discussions about a subordinate's performance tend to come high on the list of workplace situations people would rather avoid, because such conversations have the potential to make both parties feel threatened or embarrassed.

Subordinates are reluctant to trigger the discussion because they are worried about coming across as thin-
skinned or whiny. Bosses tend to avoid initiating these
talks because they are concerned about the way the
subordinate might react; the discussion could force the
boss to make explicit his lack of confidence in the subordinate, in turn putting the subordinate on the defensive and making the situation worse.[2]

As a result, bosses who observe the dynamics of the
set-up-to-fail syndrome being played out may be
tempted to avoid an explicit discussion. Instead, they
will proceed tacitly by trying to encourage their perceived weak performers. That approach has the short-
term benefit of bypassing the discomfort of an open discussion, but it has three major disadvantages.

First, a one-sided approach on the part of the boss is
less likely to lead to lasting improvement because it
focuses on only one symptom of the problem—the
boss's behavior. It does not address the subordinate's
role in the underperformance.

Second, even if the boss's encouragement were successful in improving the employee's performance, a unilateral approach would limit what both he and the subordinate could otherwise learn from a more up-front
handling of the problem. The subordinate, in particular,
would not have the benefit of observing and learning
from how his boss handled the difficulties in their relationship—problems the subordinate may come across
someday with the people he manages.

Finally, bosses trying to modify their behavior in a
unilateral way often end up going overboard; they suddenly give the subordinate more autonomy and responsibility than he can handle productively. Predictably, the
subordinate fails to deliver to the boss's satisfaction,

which leaves the boss even more frustrated and convinced that the subordinate cannot function without
intense supervision.

We are not saying that intervention is always the best
course of action. Sometimes, intervention is not possible
or desirable. There may be, for instance, overwhelming
evidence that the subordinate is not capable of doing his
job. He was a hiring or promotion mistake, which is best
handled by removing him from the position. In other
cases, the relationship
between the boss and
the subordinate is too far
gone—too much damage
has occurred to repair it.
And finally, sometimes
bosses are too busy and under too much pressure to invest the kind of resources that intervention involves.

The boss must separate emotion from reality: Is the subordinate really as bad as I think he is?

Yet often the biggest obstacle to effective intervention is the boss's mind-set. When a boss believes that a
subordinate is a weak performer and, on top of everything else, that person also aggravates him, he is not
going to be able to cover up his feelings with words; his
underlying convictions will come out in the meeting.
That is why preparation for the intervention is crucial.
Before even deciding to have a meeting, the boss must
separate emotion from reality. Was the situation always
as bad as it is now? Is the subordinate really as bad as I
think he is? What is the hard evidence I have for that
belief? Could there be other factors, aside from performance, that have led me to label this subordinate a weak
performer? Aren't there a few things that he does well?
He must have displayed above-average qualifications
when we decided to hire him. Did these qualifications
evaporate all of a sudden?

The boss might even want to mentally play out part of the conversation beforehand. If I say this to the subordinate, what might he answer? Yes, sure, he would say that it was not his fault and that the customer was unreasonable. Those excuses—are they really without merit? Could he have a point? Could it be that, under other circumstances, I might have looked more favorably upon them? And if I still believe I'm right, how can I help the subordinate see things more clearly?

The boss must also mentally prepare himself to be open to the subordinate's views, even if the subordinate challenges him about any evidence regarding his poor performance. It will be easier for the boss to be open if, when preparing for the meeting, he has already challenged his own preconceptions.

Even when well prepared, bosses typically experience some degree of discomfort during intervention meetings. That is not all bad. The subordinate will probably be somewhat uncomfortable as well, and it is reassuring for him to see that his boss is a human being, too.

Calculating Costs and Benefits

As we've said, an intervention is not always advisable. But when it is, it results in a range of outcomes that are uniformly better than the alternative—that is, continued underperformance and tension. After all, bosses who systematically choose either to ignore their subordinates' underperformance or to opt for the more expedient solution of simply removing perceived weak performers are condemned to keep repeating the same mistakes. Finding and training replacements for perceived weak performers is a costly and recurrent expense. So is monitoring and controlling the deteriorating performance of a disenchanted subordinate. Getting results *in spite of* one's staff is not a sustainable solution. In other words, it makes sense to think of the intervention as an investment, not an expense—with the payback likely to be high.

How high that payback will be and what form it will take obviously depend on the outcome of the intervention, which will itself depend not only on the quality of the intervention but also on several key contextual factors: How long has that relationship been spiraling downward? Does the subordinate have the intellectual and emotional resources to make the effort that will be required? Does the boss have enough time and energy to do his part?

We have observed outcomes that can be clustered into three categories. In the best-case scenario, the intervention leads to a mixture of coaching, training, job redesign, and a clearing of the air; as a result, the relationship and the subordinate's performance improve, and the costs associated with the syndrome go away or, at least, decrease measurably.

In the second-best scenario, the subordinate's performance improves only marginally, but because the subordinate received an honest and open hearing from the boss, the relationship between the two becomes more productive. Boss and subordinate develop a better understanding of those job dimensions the subordinate can do well and those he struggles with. This improved understanding leads the boss and the subordinate to explore *together* how they can develop a better fit between the job and the subordinate's strengths and weaknesses. That improved fit can be achieved by significantly modifying the subordinate's existing job or by transferring the subordinate to another job within the company. It may even result in the subordinate's choosing to leave the company.

While that outcome is not as successful as the first one, it is still productive; a more honest relationship eases the strain on both the boss and the subordinate, and in turn on the subordinate's subordinates. If the subordinate moves to a new job within the organization that better suits him, he will likely become a stronger performer. His relocation may also open up a spot in his old job for a better performer. The key point is that, having been treated fairly, the subordinate is much more likely to accept the outcome of the process. Indeed, recent studies show that the perceived fairness of a process has a major impact on employees' reactions to its outcomes. (See "Fair Process: Managing in the Knowledge Economy," by W. Chan Kim and Renée Mauborgne, HBR July–August 1997.)

Such fairness is a benefit even in the cases where, despite the boss's best efforts, neither the subordinate's performance nor his relationship with his boss improves significantly. Sometimes this happens: the subordinate truly lacks the ability to meet the job requirements, he has no interest in making the effort to improve, and the boss and the subordinate have both professional and personal differences that are irreconcilable. In those cases, however, the intervention still yields indirect benefits because, even if termination follows, other employees within the company are less likely to feel expendable or betrayed when they see that the subordinate received fair treatment.

Prevention Is the Best Medicine

The set-up-to-fail syndrome is not an organizational fait accompli. It can be unwound. The first step is for the boss to become aware of its existence and acknowledge the possibility that he might be part of the problem. The second step requires that the boss initiate a clear, focused intervention. Such an intervention demands an open exchange between the boss and the subordinate based on the evidence of poor performance, its underlying causes, and their joint responsibilities— culminating in a joint decision on how to work toward eliminating the syndrome itself.

> *The set-up-to-fail syndrome can be unwound. Reversing it requires managers to challenge their own assumptions.*

Reversing the syndrome requires managers to challenge their own assumptions. It also demands that they have the courage to look within themselves for causes and solutions before placing the burden of responsibility where it does not fully belong. Prevention of the syndrome, however, is clearly the best option.

In our current research, we examine prevention directly. Our results are still preliminary, but it appears that bosses who manage to consistently avoid the set-up-to-fail syndrome have several traits in common. They do not, interestingly, behave the same way with all subordinates. They are more involved with some subordinates than others—they even monitor some subordinates more than others. However, they do so without disempowering and discouraging subordinates.

How? One answer is that those managers begin by being actively involved with all their employees, gradually reducing their involvement based on improved performance. Early guidance is not threatening to subordinates, because it is not triggered by performance shortcomings; it is systematic and meant to help set the conditions for future success. Frequent contact in the beginning of the relationship gives the boss ample opportunity to communicate with subordinates about priorities, performance measures, time allocation, and even expectations of the type and frequency of communication. That kind of clarity goes a long way toward preventing the dynamic of the set-up-to-fail syndrome, which is so often fueled by unstated expectations and a lack of clarity about priorities.

For example, in the case of Steve and Jeff, Jeff could have made explicit very early on that he wanted Steve to set up a system that would analyze the root causes of quality control rejections systematically. He could have explained the benefits of establishing such a system during the initial stages of setting up the new production line, and he might have expressed his intention to be actively involved in the system's design and early operation. His future involvement might then have decreased in such a way that could have been jointly agreed on at that stage.

Another way managers appear to avoid the set-up-to-fail syndrome is by challenging their own assumptions and attitudes about employees on an ongoing basis. They work hard at resisting the temptation to categorize employees in simplistic ways. They also monitor their own reasoning. For example, when feeling frustrated about a subordinate's performance, they ask themselves, "What are the facts?" They examine whether they are expecting things from the employee that have not been articulated, and they try to be objective about how often and to what extent the employee has really failed. In other words, these bosses delve into their own assumptions and behavior before they initiate a full-blown intervention.

Finally, managers avoid the set-up-to-fail syndrome by creating an environment in which employees feel comfortable discussing their performance and their relationships with the boss. Such an environment is a function of several factors: the boss's openness, his comfort level with having his own opinions challenged, even his sense of humor. The net result is that the boss and the subordinate feel free to communicate frequently and to ask one another questions about their respective behaviors before problems mushroom or ossify.

The methods used to head off the set-up-to-fail syndrome do, admittedly, involve a great deal of emotional investment from bosses—just as interventions do. We believe, however, that this higher emotional involvement is the key to getting subordinates to work to their full potential. As with most things in life, you can only expect to get a lot back if you put a lot in. As a senior executive once said to us, "The respect you give is the respect you get." We concur. If you want—indeed, need—the people in your organization to devote their whole hearts and minds to their work, then you must, too.

About the Research

THIS ARTICLE IS BASED ON TWO STUDIES designed to understand better the causal relationship between leadership style and subordinate performance—in other words, to explore how bosses and subordinates mutually influence each other's behavior. The first study, which comprised surveys, interviews, and observations, involved 50 boss-subordinate pairs in four manufacturing operations in *Fortune* 100 companies. The second study, involving an informal survey of about 850 senior managers attending INSEAD executive-development programs over the last three years, was done to test and refine the findings generated by the first study. The executives in the second study represented a wide diversity of nationalities, industries, and personal backgrounds.

Notes

1. The influence of expectations on performance has been observed in numerous experiments by Dov Eden and his colleagues. See Dov Eden, "Leadership and Expectations: Pygmalion Effects and Other Self-filling Prophecies in Organizations," *Leadsership Quarterly*, Winter 1992, vol.3, no. 4, pp. 271–305.

2. Chris Argyris has written extensively on how and why people tend to behave unproductivly in situations they see as threatening or embarrassing. See, for example, *Knowledge for Action: A Guide to Overcoming Barriers to Organizational Change* (San Francisco: Jossey-Bass, 1993).

Originally published in March–April 1998
Reprint 98209

The Necessary Art of Persuasion

JAY A. CONGER

Executive Summary

BUSINESS TODAY IS LARGELY RUN by teams and populated by authority-averse baby boomers and Generation Xers. That makes persuasion more important than ever as a managerial tool.

But contrary to popular belief, the author asserts, persuasion is not the same as selling an idea or convincing opponents to see things your way. It is instead a process of learning from others and negotiating a shared solution. To that end, persuasion consists of four essential elements: establishing credibility, framing to find common ground, providing vivid evidence, and connecting emotionally.

Credibility grows, the author says, out of two sources: expertise and relationships. The former is a function of product or process knowledge and the latter a history of listening to and working in the best interest of others.

But even if a persuader's credibility is high, his position must make sense—even more, it must appeal—to the audience. Therefore, a persuader must frame his position to illuminate its benefits to everyone who will feel its impact.

Persuasion then becomes a matter of presenting evidence—but not just ordinary charts and spreadsheets. The author says the most effective persuaders use vivid—even over-the-top—stories, metaphors, and examples to make their positions come alive.

Finally, good persuaders have the ability to accurately sense and respond to their audience's emotional state. Sometimes, that means they have to suppress their own emotions; at other times, they must intensify them.

Persuasion can be a force for enormous good in an organization, but people must understand it for what it is: an often painstaking process that requires insight, planning, and compromise.

IF THERE EVER WAS A TIME FOR BUSINESSPEOPLE to learn the fine art of persuasion, it is now. Gone are the command-and-control days of executives managing by decree. Today businesses are run largely by cross-functional teams of peers and populated by baby boomers and their Generation X offspring, who show little tolerance for unquestioned authority. Electronic communication and globalization have further eroded the traditional hierarchy, as ideas and people flow more freely than ever around organizations and as decisions get made closer to the markets. These fundamental changes, more than a decade in the making but now firmly part of the economic landscape, essentially come down to this: work today gets done in an environment where people don't just ask What should I do? but Why should I do it?

To answer this why question effectively is to persuade. Yet many businesspeople misunderstand persuasion, and more still underutilize it. The reason? Persuasion is widely perceived as a skill reserved for selling products and closing deals. It is also commonly seen as just another form of manipulation—devious and to be avoided. Certainly, persuasion can be used in selling and deal-clinching situations, and it can be misused to manipulate people. But exercised constructively and to its full potential, persuasion supersedes sales and is quite the opposite of deception. Effective persuasion becomes a negotiating and learning process through which a persuader leads colleagues to a problem's shared solution. Persuasion does indeed involve moving people to a position they don't currently hold, but not by begging or cajoling. Instead, it involves careful preparation, the proper framing of arguments, the presentation of vivid supporting evidence, and the effort to find the correct emotional match with your audience.

Effective persuasion is a difficult and time-consuming proposition, but it may also be more powerful than the command-and-control managerial model it succeeds. As AlliedSignal's CEO Lawrence Bossidy said recently, "The day when you could yell and scream and beat people into good performance is over. Today you have to appeal to them by helping them see how they can get from here to there, by establishing some credibility, and by giving them some reason and help to get there. Do all those things, and they'll knock down doors." In essence, he is describing persuasion—now more than ever, the language of business leadership.

Think for a moment of your definition of persuasion. If you are like most businesspeople I have encountered, you see persuasion as a relatively straightforward process (See "Twelve Years of Watching and Listening," on page 252). First, you strongly state your position. Second, you outline the supporting arguments, followed by a highly assertive, data-based exposition. Finally, you enter the deal-making stage and work toward a "close." In other words, you use logic, persistence, and personal enthusiasm to get others to buy a good idea. The reality is that following this process is one surefire way to fail at persuasion. (See "Four Ways Not to Persuade," on page 253.)

What, then, constitutes effective persuasion? If persuasion is a learning and negotiating process, then in the most general terms it involves phases of discovery, preparation, and dialogue. Getting ready to persuade colleagues can take weeks or months of planning as you learn about your audience and the position you intend to argue. Before they even start to talk, effective persuaders have considered their positions from every angle. What investments in time and money will my position require from others? Is my supporting evidence weak in any way? Are there alternative positions I need to examine?

Dialogue happens before and during the persuasion process. Before the process begins, effective persuaders use dialogue to learn more about their audience's opinions, concerns, and perspectives. During the process, dialogue continues to be a form of learning, but it is also the beginning of the negotiation stage. You invite people to discuss, even debate, the merits of your position, and then to offer honest feedback and suggest alternative solutions. That may sound like a slow way to achieve your goal, but effective persuasion is about testing and revising ideas in concert with your colleagues' concerns and needs. In fact, the best persuaders not only listen to others but also incorporate their perspectives into a shared solution.

Persuasion, in other words, often involves —indeed, demands—compromise. Perhaps that is why the most effective persuaders seem to share a common trait: they are open-minded, never dogmatic. They enter the persuasion process prepared to adjust their viewpoints and incorporate others' ideas. That approach to persuasion is, interestingly, highly persuasive in itself. When colleagues see that a persuader is eager to hear their views and willing to make changes in response to their needs and concerns, they respond very positively. They trust the persuader more and listen more attentively. They don't fear being bowled over or manipulated. They see the persuader as flexible and are thus more willing to make sacrifices themselves. Because that is such a powerful dynamic, good persuaders often enter the persuasion process with judicious compromises already prepared.

Four Essential Steps

Effective persuasion involves four distinct and essential steps. First, effective persuaders establish credibility. Second, they frame their goals in a way that identifies common ground with those they intend to persuade. Third, they reinforce their positions using vivid language and compelling evidence. And fourth, they connect emotionally with their audience. As one of the most effective

executives in our research commented, "The most valuable lesson I've learned about persuasion over the years
is that there's just as much strategy in how you present
your position as in the position itself. In fact, I'd say the
strategy of presentation is the more critical."

ESTABLISH CREDIBILITY

The first hurdle persuaders must overcome is their own
credibility. A persuader can't advocate a new or contrarian position without having people wonder, Can we trust
this individual's perspectives and opinions? Such a reaction is understandable.
After all, allowing oneself
to be persuaded is risky,
because any new initiative
demands a commitment
of time and resources. Yet
even though persuaders

*Research strongly suggests
that most managers are in
the habit of overestimating
their own credibility—
often considerably.*

must have high credibility, our research strongly suggests
that most managers overestimate their own credibility—
considerably.

In the workplace, credibility grows out of two
sources: expertise and relationships. People are considered to have high levels of expertise if they have a history
of sound judgment or have proven themselves knowledgeable and well informed about their proposals. For
example, in proposing a new product idea, an effective
persuader would need to be perceived as possessing a
thorough understanding of the product—its specifica-
tions, target markets, customers, and competing products. A history of prior successes would further
strengthen the persuader's perceived expertise. One
extremely successful executive in our research had a

track record of 14 years of devising highly effective advertising campaigns. Not surprisingly, he had an easy time winning colleagues over to his position. Another manager had a track record of seven successful new-product launches in a period of five years. He, too, had an advantage when it came to persuading his colleagues to support his next new idea.

On the relationship side, people with high credibility have demonstrated—again, usually over time—that they can be trusted to listen and to work in the best interests of others. They have also consistently shown strong emotional character and integrity; that is, they are not known for mood extremes or inconsistent performance. Indeed, people who are known to be honest, steady, and reliable have an edge when going into any persuasion situation. Because their relationships are robust, they are more apt to be given the benefit of the doubt. One effective persuader in our research was considered by colleagues to be remarkably trustworthy and fair; many people confided in her. In addition, she generously shared credit for good ideas and provided staff with exposure to the company's senior executives. This woman had built strong relationships, which meant her staff and peers were always willing to consider seriously what she proposed.

If expertise and relationships determine credibility, it is crucial that you undertake an honest assessment of where you stand on both criteria before beginning to persuade. To do so, first step back and ask yourself the following questions related to expertise: How will others perceive my knowledge about the strategy, product, or change I am proposing? Do I have a track record in this area that others know about and respect? Then, to assess the strength of your relationship credibility, ask yourself, Do those I am hoping to persuade see me as helpful, trustworthy, and supportive? Will they see me as someone in sync with them—emotionally, intellectually, and politically—on issues like this one? Finally, it is important to note that it is not enough to get your own read on these matters. You must also test your answers with colleagues you trust to give you a reality check. Only then will you have a complete picture of your credibility.

A persuader should make a concerted effort to meet one-on-one with all the key people he or she plans to persuade.

In most cases, that exercise helps people discover that they have some measure of weakness, either on the expertise or on the relationship side of credibility. The challenge then becomes to fill in such gaps.

In general, if your area of weakness is on the expertise side, you have several options:

- First, you can learn more about the complexities of your position through either formal or informal education and through conversations with knowledgeable individuals. You might also get more relevant experience on the job by asking, for instance, to be assigned to a team that would increase your insight into particular markets or products.

- Another alternative is to hire someone to bolster your expertise—for example, an industry consultant or a recognized outside expert, such as a professor. Either one may have the knowledge and experience required to support your position effectively. Similarly, you may tap experts within your organization to advocate your position. Their credibility becomes a substitute for your own.

- You can also utilize other outside sources of information to support your position, such as respected business or trade periodicals, books, independently produced reports, and lectures by experts. In our research, one executive from the clothing industry successfully persuaded his company to reposition an entire product line to a more youthful market after bolstering his credibility with articles by a noted demographer in two highly regarded journals and with two independent market-research studies.

- Finally, you may launch pilot projects to demonstrate on a small scale your expertise and the value of your ideas.

As for filling in the relationship gap:

- You should make a concerted effort to meet one-on-one with all the key people you plan to persuade. This is not the time to outline your position but rather to get a range of perspectives on the issue at hand. If you have the time and resources, you should even offer to help these people with issues that concern them.

- Another option is to involve like-minded coworkers who already have strong relationships with your audience. Again, that is a matter of seeking out substitutes on your own behalf.

For an example of how these strategies can be put to work, consider the case of a chief operating officer of a large retail bank, whom we will call Tom Smith. Although he was new to his job, Smith ardently wanted to persuade the senior management team that the company was in serious trouble. He believed that the bank's overhead was excessive and would jeopardize its position as the industry entered a more competitive era. Most of his colleagues, however, did not see the potential seriousness of the situation. Because the bank had been enormously successful in recent years, they believed changes in the industry posed little danger. In addition to being newly appointed, Smith had another problem: his career had been in financial services, and he was considered an outsider in the world of retail banking. Thus he had few personal connections to draw on as he made his case, nor was he perceived to be particularly knowledgeable about marketplace exigencies.

As a first step in establishing credibility, Smith hired an external consultant with respected credentials in the industry who showed that the bank was indeed poorly positioned to be a low-cost producer. In a series of interactive presentations to the bank's top-level management, the consultant revealed how the company's leading competitors were taking aggressive actions to contain operating costs. He made it clear from these presentations that not cutting costs would soon cause the bank to fall drastically behind the competition. These findings were then distributed in written reports that circulated throughout the bank.

Next, Smith determined that the bank's branch managers were critical to his campaign. The buy-in of those respected and informed individuals would signal to others in the company that his concerns were valid. Moreover, Smith looked to the branch managers because he believed that they could increase his expertise about marketplace trends and also help him test his own assumptions. Thus, for the next three months, he visited every branch in his region of Ontario, Canada—135 in all. During each visit, he spent time with branch managers, listening to their perceptions of the bank's strengths and weaknesses. He learned firsthand about the competition's initiatives and customer trends, and he solicited ideas for improving the bank's services and minimizing costs. By the time he was through, Smith had a broad perspective on the bank's future that few people even in senior management possessed. And he had built dozens of relationships in the process.

Finally, Smith launched some small but highly visible initiatives to demonstrate his expertise and capabilities. For example, he was concerned about slow growth in the company's mortgage business and the loan officers' resulting slip in morale. So he devised a program in which new mortgage customers would make no payments for the first 90 days. The initiative proved remarkably successful, and in short order Smith appeared to be a far more savvy retail banker than anyone had assumed.

Another example of how to establish credibility comes from Microsoft. In 1990, two product-development managers, Karen Fries and Barry Linnett, came to believe that the market would greatly welcome software that featured a "social interface." They envisioned a package that would employ animated human and animal characters to show users how to go about their computing tasks.

Inside Microsoft, however, employees had immediate concerns about the concept. Software programmers ridiculed the cute characters. Animated characters had been used before only in software for children, making their use in adult environments hard to envision. But Fries and Linnett felt their proposed product had both dynamism and complexity, and they remained convinced that consumers would eagerly buy such programs. They also believed that the home-computer software market—largely untapped at the time and with fewer software standards—would be open to such innovation.

Within the company, Fries had gained quite a bit of relationship credibility. She had started out as a recruiter for the company in 1987 and had worked directly for many of Microsoft's senior executives. They trusted and liked her. In addition, she had been responsible for hiring the company's product and program managers. As a result, she knew all the senior people at Microsoft and had hired many of the people who would be deciding on her product.

Linnett's strength laid in his expertise. In particular, he knew the technology behind an innovative tutorial program called PC Works. In addition, both Fries and Linnett had managed Publisher, a product with a unique help feature called Wizards, which Microsoft's CEO, Bill Gates, had liked. But those factors were sufficient only to get an initial hearing from Microsoft's senior management. To persuade the organization to move forward, the pair would need to improve perceptions of their expertise. It hurt them that this type of social-interface software had no proven track record of success and that they were both novices with such software. Their challenge became one of finding substitutes for their own expertise.

Their first step was a wise one. From within Microsoft, they hired respected technical guru Darrin Massena. With Massena, they developed a set of prototypes to demonstrate that they did indeed understand the software's technology and could make it work. They then tested the prototypes in market research, and users responded enthusiastically. Finally, and most important, they enlisted two Stanford University professors, Clifford

Nass and Bryon Reeves, both experts in human-computer interaction. In several meetings with Microsoft senior managers and Gates himself, they presented a rigorously compiled and thorough body of research that demonstrated how and why social-interface software was ideally suited to the average computer user. In addition, Fries and Linnett asserted that considerable jumps in computing power would make more realistic cartoon characters an increasingly malleable technology. Their product, they said, was the leading edge of an incipient software revolution. Convinced, Gates approved a full product-development team, and in January 1995, the product called BOB was launched. BOB went on to sell more than half a million copies, and its concept and technology are being used within Microsoft as a platform for developing several Internet products.

Credibility is the cornerstone of effective persuading; without it, a persuader won't be given the time of day. In the best-case scenario, people enter into a persuasion situation with some measure of expertise and relationship credibility. But it is important to note that credibility along either lines can be built or bought. Indeed, it must be, or the next steps are an exercise in futility.

FRAME FOR COMMON GROUND

Even if your credibility is high, your position must still appeal strongly to the people you are trying to persuade. After all, few people will jump on board a train that will bring them to ruin or even mild discomfort. Effective persuaders must be adept at describing their positions in terms that illuminate their advantages. As any parent can tell you, the fastest way to get a child to come along willingly on a trip to the grocery store is to point out that there are lollipops by the cash register. That is not deception. It is just a persuasive way of framing the benefits of taking such a journey. In work situations, persuasive framing is obviously more complex, but the underlying principle is the same. It is a process of identifying shared benefits.

Monica Ruffo, an account executive for an advertising agency, offers a good example of persuasive framing. Her client, a fast-food chain, was instituting a promotional campaign in Canada; menu items such as a hamburger, fries, and cola were to be bundled together and sold at a low price. The strategy made sense to corporate headquarters. Its research showed that consumers thought the company's products were higher priced than the competition's, and the company was anxious to overcome this perception. The franchisees, on the other hand, were still experiencing strong sales and were far more concerned about the short-term impact that the new, low prices would have on their profit margins.

When a fast-food chain needed to persuade its franchisees to buy into a meal-pricing plan that had the potential to eat into profits, headquarters framed the initiative to accent the positive.

A less experienced persuader would have attempted to rationalize headquarters' perspective to the franchisees—to convince them of its validity. But Ruffo framed the change in pricing to demonstrate its benefits to the franchisees themselves. The new value campaign, she explained, would actually improve franchisees' profits. To back up this point, she drew on several sources. A pilot project in Tennessee, for instance, had demonstrated that under the new pricing scheme, the sales of french fries and drinks—the two most profitable items on the menu—had markedly increased. In addition, the company had rolled out medium-sized meal packages in 80% of its U.S. outlets, and franchisees' sales of fries and drinks had jumped 26%. Citing research from a respected business periodical, Ruffo also showed that when customers raised their estimate of the value they receive from a retail establishment by 10%, the establishment's sales rose by 1%. She had estimated that the new meal plan would increase value perceptions by 100%, with the result that franchisee sales could be expected to grow 10%.

Ruffo closed her presentation with a letter written many years before by the company's founder to the organization. It was an emotional letter extolling the values of the company and stressing the importance of the franchisees to the company's success. It also highlighted the importance of the company's position as the low-price

In some situations, no shared advantages are readily apparent. In these cases, effective persuaders adjust their positions.

leader in the industry. The beliefs and values contained in the letter had long been etched in the minds of Ruffo's audience. Hearing them again only confirmed the company's concern for the franchisees and the importance of their winning formula. They also won Ruffo a standing ovation. That day, the franchisees voted unanimously to support the new meal-pricing plan.

The Ruffo case illustrates why—in choosing appropriate positioning—it is critical first to identify your objective's tangible benefits to the people you are trying to persuade. Sometimes that is easy. Mutual benefits exist. In other situations, however, no shared advantages are readily apparent—or meaningful. In these cases, effective persuaders adjust their positions. They know it is impossible to engage people and gain commitment to ideas or plans without highlighting the advantages to all the parties involved.

At the heart of framing is a solid understanding of your audience. Even before starting to persuade, the best persuaders we have encountered closely study the issues that matter to their colleagues. They use conversations, meetings, and other forms of dialogue to collect essential information. They are good at listening. They test their ideas with trusted confidants, and they ask questions of the people they will later be persuading. Those steps help them think through the arguments, the evidence, and the perspectives they will present. Oftentimes, this process causes them to alter or compromise their own plans before they even start persuading. It is through this thoughtful, inquisitive approach they develop frames that appeal to their audience.

Consider the case of a manager who was in charge of process engineering for a jet engine manufacturer. He had redesigned the work flow for routine turbine maintenance for airline clients in a manner that would dramatically shorten the turnaround time for servicing. Before presenting his ideas to the company's president, he consulted a good friend in the company, the vice president of engineering, who knew the president well. This conversation revealed that the president's prime concern would not be speed or efficiency but profitability. To get the president's buy-in, the vice president explained, the new system would have to improve the company's profitability in the short run by lowering operating expenses.

At first this information had the manager stumped. He had planned to focus on efficiency and had even intended to request additional funding to make the process work. But his conversation with the vice president sparked him to change his position. Indeed, he went so far as to change the work-flow design itself so that it no longer required new investment but rather drove down costs. He then carefully documented the cost savings and profitability gains that his new plan would produce and presented this revised plan to the president. With his initiative positioned anew, the manager persuaded the president and got the project approved.

PROVIDE EVIDENCE

With credibility established and a common frame identified, persuasion becomes a matter of presenting evidence. Ordinary evidence, however, won't do. We have found that the most effective persuaders use language in a particular way. They supplement numerical data with examples, stories, metaphors, and analogies to make their positions come alive. That use of language paints a vivid word picture and, in doing so, lends a compelling and tangible quality to the persuader's point of view.

Numbers do not make an emotional impact, but stories and vivid language do.

Think about a typical persuasion situation. The persuader is often advocating a goal, strategy, or initiative with an uncertain outcome. Karen Fries and Barry Linnett, for instance, wanted Microsoft to invest millions of dollars in a software package with chancy technology and unknown market demand. The team could have supported its case solely with market research, financial projections, and the like. But that would have been a mistake, because research shows that most people perceive such reports as not entirely informative. They are too abstract to be completely meaningful or memorable. In essence, the numbers don't make an emotional impact.

By contrast, stories and vivid language do, particularly when they present comparable situations to the one under discussion. A marketing manager trying to persuade senior executives to invest in a new product, for example, might cite examples of similar investments that paid off handsomely. Indeed, we found that people readily draw lessons from such cases. More important, the research shows that listeners absorb information in proportion to its vividness. Thus it is no wonder that Fries and Linnett hit a home run when they presented their case for BOB with the following analogy:

> *Imagine you want to cook dinner and you must first go to the supermarket. You have all the flexibility you want—you can cook anything in the world as long as you know how and have the time and desire to do it. When you arrive at the supermarket, you find all these overstuffed aisles with cryptic single-word headings like "sundries" and "ethnic food" and "condiments." These are the menus on typical computer interfaces. The question is whether salt is under condiments or ethnic food or near the potato chip section. There are surrounding racks and wall spaces, much as our software interfaces now have support buttons, tool bars, and lines around the perimeters. Now after you have collected everything, you still need to put it all together in the correct order to*

*make a meal. If you're a good cook, your meal will prob-
ably be good. If you're a novice, it probably won't be.*

*We [at Microsoft] have been selling under the super-
market category for years, and we think there is a big
opportunity for restaurants. That's what we are trying to
do now with BOB: pushing the next step with software
that is more like going to a restaurant, so the user
doesn't spend all of his time searching for the ingredients. We find and put the ingredients together. You sit
down, you get comfortable. We bring you a menu. We do
the work, you relax. It's an enjoyable experience. No
walking around lost trying to find things, no cooking.*

Had Fries and Linnett used a literal description of
BOB's advantages, few of their highly computer-literate
colleagues at Microsoft would have personally related to
the menu-searching frustration that BOB was designed
to eliminate. The analogy they selected, however, made
BOB's purpose both concrete and memorable.

A master persuader, Mary Kay Ash, the founder of
Mary Kay Cosmetics, regularly draws on analogies to
illustrate and "sell" the business conduct she values.
Consider this speech at the company's annual sales convention:

*Back in the days of the Roman Empire, the legions of the
emperor conquered the known world. There was, however, one band of people that the Romans never conquered. Those people were the followers of the great
teacher from Bethlehem. Historians have long since discovered that one of the reasons for the sturdiness of this
folk was their habit of meeting together weekly. They
shared their difficulties, and they stood side by side.
Does this remind you of something? The way we stand*

*side by side and share our knowledge and difficulties
with each other in our weekly unit meetings? I have so
often observed when a director or unit member is con-
fronted with a personal problem that the unit stands
together in helping that sister in distress. What a won-
derful circle of friendships we have. Perhaps it's one of
the greatest fringe benefits of our company.*

Through her vivid analogy, Ash links collective support in the company to a courageous period in Christian
history. In doing so, she accomplishes several objectives.
First, she drives home her belief that collective support
is crucial to the success of the organization. Most Mary
Kay salespeople are independent operators who face the
daily challenges of direct selling. An emotional support
system of fellow salespeople is essential to ensure that
self-esteem and confidence remain intact in the face of
rejection. Next she suggests by her analogy that solidarity against the odds is the best way to stymie powerful
oppressors—to wit, the competition. Finally, Ash's
choice of analogy imbues a sense of a heroic mission to
the work of her sales force.

You probably don't need to invoke the analogy of the
Christian struggle to support your position, but effective
persuaders are not afraid of unleashing the immense
power of language. In fact, they use it to their utmost
advantage.

CONNECT EMOTIONALLY

In the business world, we like to think that our colleagues use reason to make their decisions, yet if we
scratch below the surface we will always find emotions
at play. Good persuaders are aware of the primacy of

emotions and are responsive to them in two important ways. First, they show their own emotional commitment to the position they are advocating. Such expression is a delicate matter. If you act too emotional, people may doubt your clear-headedness. But you must also show that your commitment to a goal is not

A persuader must match his or her emotional fervor to the audience's ability to receive the message.

just in your mind but in your heart and gut as well. Without this demonstration of feeling, people may wonder if you actually believe in the position you're championing.

Perhaps more important, however, is that effective persuaders have a strong and accurate sense of their audience's emotional state, and they adjust the tone of their arguments accordingly. Sometimes that means coming on strong, with forceful points. Other times, a whisper may be all that is required. The idea is that whatever your position, you match your emotional fervor to your audience's ability to receive the message.

Effective persuaders seem to have a second sense about how their colleagues have interpreted past events in the organization and how they will probably interpret a proposal. The best persuaders in our study would usually canvass key individuals who had a good pulse on the mood and emotional expectations of those about to be persuaded. They would ask those individuals how various proposals might affect colleagues on an emotional level—in essence, testing possible reactions. They were also quite effective at gathering information through informal conversations in the hallways or at lunch. In the end, their aim was to ensure that the emotional appeal behind their persuasion matched what their audience was already feeling or expecting.

To illustrate the importance of emotional matchmaking in persuasion, consider this example. The president of an aeronautics manufacturing company strongly believed that the maintenance costs and turnaround time of the company's U.S. and foreign competitors were so much better than his own company's that it stood to lose customers and profits. He wanted to communicate his fear and his urgent desire for change to his senior managers. So one afternoon, he called them into the boardroom. On an overhead screen was the projected image of a smiling man flying an old-fashioned biplane with his scarf blowing in the wind. The right half of the transparency was covered. When everyone was seated, the president explained that he felt as this pilot did, given the company's recent good fortune. The organization, after all, had just finished its most successful year in history. But then with a deep sigh, he announced that his happiness was quickly vanishing. As the president lifted the remaining portion of the sheet, he revealed an image of the pilot flying directly into a wall. The president then faced his audience and in a heavy voice said, "This is what I see happening to us." He asserted that the company was headed for a crash if people didn't take action fast. He then went on to lecture the group about the steps needed to counter this threat.

The reaction from the group was immediate and negative. Directly after the meeting, managers gathered in small clusters in the hallways to talk about the president's "scare tactics." They resented what they perceived to be the president's overstatement of the case. As the managers saw it, they had exerted enormous effort that year to break the company's records in sales and profitability. They were proud of their achievements. In fact, they had entered the meeting expecting it would be the moment of recognition. But to their absolute surprise, they were scolded.

The president's mistake? First, he should have canvassed a few members of his senior team to ascertain the emotional state of the group. From that, he would have learned that they were in need of thanks and recognition. He should then have held a separate session devoted simply to praising the team's accomplishments. Later, in a second meeting, he could have expressed his own anxieties about the coming year. And rather than blame the team for ignoring the future, he could have calmly described what he saw as emerging threats to the company and then asked his management team to help him develop new initiatives.

Now let us look at someone who found the right emotional match with his audience: Robert Marcell, head of Chrysler's small-car design team. In the early 1990s, Chrysler was eager to produce a new subcompact—indeed, the company had not introduced a new model of this type since 1978. But senior managers at Chrysler did not want to go it alone. They thought an alliance with a foreign manufacturer would improve the car's design and protect Chrysler's cash stores.

Marcell was convinced otherwise. He believed that the company should bring the design and production of a new subcompact in-house. He knew that persuading senior managers would be difficult, but he also had his own team to contend with. Team members had lost their confidence that they would ever again have the opportunity to create a good car. They were also angry that the United States had once again given up its position to foreign competitors when it came to small cars.

Marcell decided that his persuasion tactics had to be built around emotional themes that would touch his audience. From innumerable conversations around the company, he learned that many people felt as he did—that to surrender the subcompact's design to a foreign manufacturer was to surrender the company's soul and, ultimately, its ability to provide jobs. In addition, he felt deeply that his organization was a talented group hungry for a challenge and an opportunity to restore its self-esteem and pride. He would need to demonstrate his faith in the team's abilities.

Marcell prepared a 15-minute talk built around slides of his hometown, Iron River, a now defunct mining town in Upper Michigan, devastated, in large part, by foreign mining companies. On the screen flashed recent photographs he had taken of his boarded-up high school, the shuttered homes of his childhood friends, the crumbling ruins of the town's ironworks, closed churches, and an abandoned railroad yard. After a description of each of these places, he said the phrase, "We couldn't compete"—like the refrain of a hymn. Marcell's point was that the same outcome awaited Detroit if the production of small cars was not brought back to the United States. Surrender was the enemy, he said, and devastation would follow if the group did not take immediate action.

Marcell ended his slide show on a hopeful note. He spoke of his pride in his design group and then challenged the team to build a "made-in-America" subcompact that would prove that the United States could still compete. The speech, which echoed the exact sentiments of the audience, rekindled the group's fighting spirit. Shortly after the speech, group members began drafting their ideas for a new car.

Marcell then took his slide show to the company's senior management and ultimately to Chrysler chairman

Lee Iacocca. As Marcell showed his slides, he could see that Iacocca was touched. Iacocca, after all, was a fighter and a strongly patriotic man himself. In fact, Marcell's approach was not too different from Iacocca's earlier appeal to the United States Congress to save Chrysler. At the end of the show, Marcell stopped and said, "If we dare to be different, we could be the reason the U.S. auto industry survives. We could be the reason our kids and grandkids don't end up working at fast-food chains." Iacocca stayed on for two hours as Marcell explained in greater detail what his team was planning. Afterward, Iacocca changed his mind and gave Marcell's group approval to develop a car, the Neon.

With both groups, Marcell skillfully matched his emotional tenor to that of the group he was addressing. The ideas he conveyed resonated deeply with his largely Midwestern audience. And rather than leave them in a depressed state, he offered them hope, which was more persuasive than promising doom. Again, this played to the strong patriotic sentiments of his American-heartland audience.

No effort to persuade can succeed without emotion, but showing too much emotion can be as unproductive as showing too little. The important point to remember is that you must match your emotions to your audience's.

The Force of Persuasion

The concept of persuasion, like that of power, often confuses and even mystifies businesspeople. It is so complex—and so dangerous when mishandled—that many would rather just avoid it altogether. But like power, persuasion can be a force for enormous good in an organization. It can pull people together, move ideas forward, galvanize change, and forge constructive solu-

It's important for people to understand persuasion for what it is—not convincing and selling but learning and negotiating.

tions. To do all that, however, people must understand persuasion for what it is—not convincing and selling but learning and negotiating. Furthermore, it must be seen as an art form that requires commitment and practice, especially as today's business contingencies make persuasion more necessary than ever.

Twelve Years of Watching and Listening

THE IDEAS BEHIND THIS ARTICLE spring from three streams of research.

For the last 12 years as both an academic and as a consultant, I have been studying 23 senior business leaders who have shown themselves to be effective change agents. Specifically, I have investigated how these individuals use language to motivate their employees, articulate vision and strategy, and mobilize their organizations to adapt to challenging business environments.

Four years ago, I started a second stream of research exploring the capabilities and characteristics of successful cross-functional team leaders. The core of my database comprised interviews with and observations of 18 individuals working in a range of U.S. and Canadian companies. These were not senior leaders as in my earlier studies but low- and middle-level managers. Along with interviewing the colleagues of these people, I also compared their skills with those of other team leaders—in particular, with the leaders of less successful cross-functional teams engaged in similar initiatives within the same companies. Again, my focus was on language, but I also studied the influence of interpersonal skills.

The similarities in the persuasion skills possessed by both the change-agent leaders and effective team leaders prompted me to explore the academic literature on persuasion and rhetoric, as well as on the art of gospel preaching. Meanwhile, to learn how most managers approach the persuasion process, I observed several dozen managers in company meetings, and I employed simulations in company executive-education programs where groups of managers had to persuade one another on hypothetical business objectives. Finally, I selected a group of 14 managers known for their outstanding abilities in constructive persuasion. For several months, I interviewed them and their colleagues and observed them in actual work situations.

Four Ways Not to Persuade

IN MY WORK WITH MANAGERS as a researcher and as a consultant, I have had the unfortunate opportunity to see executives fail miserably at persuasion. Here are the four most common mistakes people make:

1. They attempt to make their case with an up-front, hard sell. I call this the John Wayne approach. Managers strongly state their position at the outset, and then through a process of persistence, logic, and exuberance, they try to push the idea to a close. In reality, setting out a strong position at the start of a persuasion effort gives potential opponents something to grab onto—and fight against. It's far better to present your position with the finesse and reserve of a lion tamer, who engages his "partner" by showing him the legs of a chair. In other words, effective persuaders don't begin the process by giving their colleagues a clear target in which to set their jaws.

2. They resist compromise. Too many managers see compromise as surrender, but it is essential to constructive persuasion. Before people buy into a proposal, they want to see that the persuader is flexible enough to respond to their concerns. Compromises can often lead to better, more sustainable shared solutions.

By not compromising, ineffective persuaders unconsciously send the message that they think persuasion is a one-way street. But persuasion is a process of give-and-take. Kathleen Reardon, a professor of organizational behavior at the University of Southern California, points out that a persuader rarely changes another person's behavior or viewpoint without altering his or her own in the process. To persuade meaningfully, we must not only listen to others but also incorporate their perspectives into our own.

3. They think the secret of persuasion lies in presenting great arguments. In persuading people to change their minds, great arguments matter. No doubt about it. But arguments, per se, are only one part of the equation. Other factors matter just as much, such as the persuader's credibility and his or her ability to create a proper, mutually beneficial frame for a position, connect on the right emotional level with an audience, and communicate through vivid language that makes arguments come alive.

4. They assume persuasion is a one-shot effort.
Persuasion is a process, not an event. Rarely, if ever, is it possible to arrive at a shared solution on the first try. More often than not, persuasion involves listening to people, testing a position, developing a new position that reflects input from the group, more testing, incorporating compromises, and then trying again. If this sounds like a slow and difficult process, that's because it is. But the results are worth the effort.

Originally published in May–June 1998
Reprint 98304

About the Contributors

MAHLON APGAR, IV is a counselor on real estate and infrastructure to major corporations and institutions. A former partner at McKinsey & Company, he has managed a consulting firm from his office since 1990.

CHRIS ARGYRIS is the James Bryant Conant Professor of Education and Organizational Behavior at Harvard University. He has consulted for numerous organizations and has served as a special consultant to the governments of England, France, Germany, Italy, and Sweden on problems of executive development and productivity. Professor Argyris is the author of 300 articles and 30 books, including *Knowledge for Action: A Guide to Overlooking Barriers to Organizational Change* and *On Organizational Learning*. In 1994, he received the Academy of Management's Award for Lifetime Contributions to the Discipline of Management.

JEAN-LOUIS BARSOUX is a research fellow at INSEAD specializing in organizational behavior, particularly cross-cultural issues. He is the coauthor, with Susan Schneider, of *Managing Across Cultures* and the coauthor, with Peter Lawrence, of *French Management: Elitism in Action* and the *Harvard Business Review* article "The Making of French Managers."

JAY A. CONGER is the executive director of the Leadership Institute, which is based at the Marshall School of Business,

University of Southern California. His research focuses on executive leadership, organizational change, the training and development of leadership, and boards of directors. He is the author of more than 60 articles and book chapters on these subjects as well as seven books. Among his most recent books are *Winning 'Em Over* and *Charismatic Leadership in Organizations*. Professor Conger was selected by *Business Week* as the best professor in the teaching of leadership to executives.

ROBIN J. ELY is an associate professor at the School of International and Public Affairs, Columbia University. Her current research focuses on how organizations can better manage their race and gender relations while simultaneously increasing their effectiveness. Previously, she has investigated the nature of professional women's experiences at work as a function of the degree to which women hold positions of power within the organization. Dr. Ely has published numerous articles in books and journals and presented her work at conferences in both the United States and Europe to academics and practitioners alike. She teaches courses in statistics and group dynamics, with a special emphasis on race, ethnicity, and gender relations as relationships of power.

ROB GOFFEE is an internationally respected authority on organizational transformation. A professor of organizational behavior and subject area chair at the London Business School since 1995, Goffee has published six books and more than 40 articles in scholarly and managerial journals, most recently the *Harvard Business Review*. Prior to joining the London Business School, he held a number of academic positions and more recently has held a visiting appointment at the Australian Graduate School of Management in Sydney. Professor Goffee is a frequent contributor to newspapers and magazines, and has appeared as a guest on many radio and television programs on business issues. In addition, he consults with a number of large corporations in the areas of organizational change, corporate culture, and management development.

GARETH JONES is the British Telecom Professor of Organizational Development at Henley. Previously, he was the senior vice president of human resources for Polygram International, one of the world's largest recorded music and film companies. His research interests are in the areas of corporate cohesion, leadership, and change. He is a visiting professor of organizational behavior at INSEAD and is the founding partner of Creative Management Association, which works internationally with companies where creativity is a key source of competitive advantage.

J. STERLING LIVINGSTON is chairman of the Sterling Institute, which he formed in 1971, after teaching for 25 years at the Harvard Business School. Recently, Dr. Livingston established a new company called Computer-Assisted Leadership, Inc. (CAL), which uses the power of the computer to help managerial leaders perfect their personal leadership practices. He has established several management consulting and education organizations, including Harbridge House, Inc.; Management Systems Corporation; the Logistic Management Institute, which he established for the Department of Defense; and the Economic Development Education Institute, which he formed for the Department of Commerce. He was the first person to document the powerful influence of a manager's expectations on the performance of subordinates.

JEAN-FRANÇOIS MANZONI is on faculty at INSEAD, where he is also an affiliate member of the Corporate Renewal initiative (CORE) and a member of the Centre for Advanced Learning Technologies (CALT). His research and consulting activities focus on the management of change at the individual and organizational levels. He is a three-time recipient of the Outstanding Teacher Award in INSEAD's MBA program.

JEFFREY PFEFFER is the Thomas D. Dee Professor of Organizational Behavior at the Stanford Graduate School of Business. He is the author of eight books, including *The Human Equation, Managing with Power,* and *Competitive Advantage through People,* all from the Harvard Business School Press. He has consulted extensively for companies, universities, and industry associations in the United States as well as in 20 other countries.

DAVID A. THOMAS is currently an associate professor of organizational behavior and human resource management at the Harvard Graduate School of Business Administration. Professor Thomas is a noted authority on mentoring, executive development, and the challenges of creating and effectively managing a diverse workforce. He is a member of the Academy of Management, National Training Laboratories, and the International Society for the Psychoanalytic Study of Organizations.

Index

ABB Asea Brown Boveri, 17
access-and-legitimacy
    paradigm, 121, 132–136
"Access Capital" (fictional
    company name), 133–136
AES Corporation, 81, 90, 93–94
affirmative action. *See* discrim-
    ination-and-fairness
    paradigm
agency theory, 80–81
Air Products and Chemicals, 89
Allen, Robert, 162
alternative workplace (AW)
    balance between work and
      home life and, 184–185,
      188
    economics of, 167–174
    factors in suitability of,
      161–166
    implementation of, 174–186
    motivations for, 156–158
    myths about, 186–189
    options in, 158–161
    senior executives' views of,
      193–196
American Express, 163, 167,

176–177, 181, 193–196
apparel industry, 84
Apple Computer, 21, 22
Arthur, Jeffrey, 76
Ash, Mary Kay, 245–246
Atkinson, John W., 56
AT&T, 156, 157, 162, 168, 169
    Creative Workplace Solu-
      tions Initiative, 158–159,
      170, 171, 189–192
    managers' expectations and,
      50, 60–61, 64
automobile industry, 82–83
AW. *See* alternative workplace

Baron, James N., 81
BBC. *See* British Broadcasting
    Company
Bennis, Warren, 69
Berlew, David E., 50, 60–61
Birt, John, 29
Boonstra, Cor, 28–29
Bossidy, Lawrence, 229
Brazzell, Stephen M., 169
British-Borneo Petroleum Syn-
    dicate, 42–44

British Broadcasting Company (BBC), 29

Camus, Albert, 208
career development, 61–63
categorical thinking, 203–207, 224–225
change. *See also* alternative workplace
  alternative workplace implementation and, 165, 175–177, 194–196
  in compensation practices, 96–97
  of corporate culture, 27–33, 81–82
  in diversity paradigm, 139–142
change programs
  alternative workplace and, 187
  empowerment and, 101, 102, 106–108, 113–119
Chenault, Kenneth I., 157
Chrysler Corporation, 69–70, 249–251
Cincinnati Milacron, 84
commitment, internal vs. external, 103–106
communal organization
  characteristics of, 21–25
  conditions appropriate to, 25–27
  example of, 42–44
communication. *See also* managers' expectations; persuasion

of high vs. low expectations, 53–55, 69–71
  response to weak employee performance and, 212–217
community. *See* corporate culture
compensation-consulting industry, 82
compensation system
  changing practices and, 96–97
  concept of compensation and, 76
  evidence on myths about, 82–91, 97–99
  fun and, 90, 99
  group-oriented basis and, 87–88, 94
  labor rates vs. costs and, 76–77, 79–80, 92, 97–98
  merit-pay and, 77–78, 80, 85–91, 92–94, 99
  myths about, 73–79, 97–99
  perpetuation of myths about, 79–82
  secrecy and, 94–95
  suggestions for approach to, 91–95
competitive strategy, and labor costs, 77, 98–99
compromise, 231, 254
conflict, and diversity, 128, 129–130, 141
corporate culture. *See also* organizational structure
  alternative workplace and,

163–164, 181–183
changing, 27–33, 81–82
communal organization
    and, 21–27
as community, 1–4, 33–34
compensation and, 81–82,
    94–95
diversity and, 131–132,
    140–142, 146–147
fragmented organization
    and, 18–21
mercenary organization
    and, 15–18
networked organization
    and, 10–14
questionnaire on, 9–10
costs
of alternative workplace,
    167–174
of labor, 76–77, 79–80, 92,
    97–99
credibility, 231, 232–239
customers, and alternative
    workplace, 168, 183–184

Dayton, Lee A., 172, 173, 176,
    186
"Delta Manufacturing" (fic-
    tional company name),
    150
Deming, W. Edwards, 86
"Dewey & Levin" (fictional
    company name), 137–138
discrimination-and-fairness
    paradigm, 121, 126–132
Disney, 16, 33
diversity

access-and-legitimacy
    paradigm and, 121,
    132–136
assumptions about, 123–124
discrimination-and-fairness
    paradigm and, 121,
    126–132
example of shifting
    paradigm and, 142–144
learning-and-effectiveness
    paradigm and, 125,
    136–139, 144–152
preconditions for paradigm
    shift and, 139–142
Dunn & Bradstreet, 164–165

East Germany, 110–111
Economist, 79
education, self-fulfilling
    prophecies in, 59–60
empowerment, 101–120
CEOs and, 109–110
change professionals and,
    113–117
diversity and, 141
effective change programs
    and, 117–119
employees and, 110–113
lack of, and change pro-
    grams, 101, 102, 106–108
prevention of failure and,
    223–225
types of commitment and,
    103–106
enthusiasm, 47
expertise, and credibility,
    232–235

external commitment
    change programs and, 108
    vs. internal commitment,
        103–106
    as survival mechanism,
        110–111

failure, patterns of, 51–53
fairness, 221–222
Fenton, Lorraine, 165
"First Interstate Bank" (fictional company name),
        142–144
Fitzgerald, Niall, 37
Ford, 63, 82–83
fragmented organization
    characteristics of, 18–20
    conditions appropriate to,
        20–21
    example of, 40–42
framing, 239–243
Frank, Robert, 81
free-rider problem, 87–88
Fries, Karen, 237–239, 243–245
fun, 90, 99

Gates, Bill, 238, 239
Geary, Brad, 185
General Motors (GM), 83, 94
Gerstner, Lou, 185
GM. *See* General Motors
goals
    attainability of, 55–57
    empowerment and, 106
Goeltz, Richard Karl, 163–164,
        167, 193–196

Haber, Alan, 177
Hall, Douglas T., 50, 60–61
Headstart program, 51
Heineken, 32
Hewlett-Packard, 23
Highland Superstores, 88
Hill, Jeffrey, 185–186
home offices, 160–161,
        165–166, 182
"hoteling," 159
House, David, 176–177,
        193–196
human relations. *See* personnel
    management

Iacocca, Lee A., 69–70, 251
IBM
    cost benefits of alternative
        workplace and, 157, 167,
        170, 172–173, 174, 175
    employees in alternative
        workplace and, 161–162,
        176, 185–186
    Mobility Initiative, 157,
        161–162, 172–174, 175
    organization at, 18, 162–163
incentive systems
    empowerment and, 111–112
    myths about pay and,
        77–78, 80, 85–91, 92–94,
        99
independent employees,
        178–179
industrial organization,
        162–163
informational organization,

162–163
in-group vs. out-group,
203–208
internal commitment
change programs and, 108
employee rewards and,
111–112
vs. external commitment,
103–106
"Iversen Dunham" (fictional
company name),
128–132, 145

James, Jill M., 158–159, 166,
168, 182, 183
Japan, and alternative workplace, 165–166
job turnover
compensation and, 78,
84–85
managers' expectations and,
65–67
work environment and,
89–90
Johnson, George, 58–59

Kelleher, Herb, 94
Komatsu, 17–18

Lancaster, Pat, 93
language
persuasion and, 243–246
power of, 81
Lantech, 93
leadership
diversity paradigm and,

122–123, 125, 140,
145–147
empowerment and, 109–110
Pygmalion effect and, 68–71
learning-and-effectiveness
paradigm, 125, 136–139
in action, 144–152
example of, 137–138
preconditions for paradigm
shift and, 139–142
shifting process and,
142–144
Life Insurance Agency Management Association, 62
Lincoln Electric, 81
Linnett, Barry, 237–239,
243–245
Lucent Technologies, 179–180,
183

machine tool industry, 83–84
Maljers, Floris, 35
managers' expectations. *See
also* set-up-to-fail syn-
drome
impact on young people,
59–64
personnel development and,
64–68
power of, 53–59
productivity and, 47–53
Pygmalion effect and,
46–47, 68–71
Marcell, Robert, 249–251
Mary Kay Cosmetics, 32,
245–246

Massena, Darrin, 238
"Mastiff" (fictional company
    name), 145–147, 150–151
"Mastiff Wear" (fictional com-
    pany name), 38–40
McClelland, David C., 56
Men's Wearhouse, 81, 85, 90
mercenary organization
    characteristics of, 15–18
    conditions appropriate to,
        17–18
    example of, 38–40
Mercer, William M., 87, 88–89
Merrill Lynch, 182
Metropolitan Life Insurance
    Company, 48–50, 63, 64
Microsoft, 237–239, 243–245
Miller, Richard S., 189–191
mission statement, 141–142
mobility paradox, 186
Moll, Albert
motivation
    extrinsic reward and, 90–91
    relation to success, 56
Motorola, 79

Nanus, Burt, 69
Nass, Clifford, 238–239
networked organization
    characteristics of, 10–14
    conditions appropriate to,
        14
    example of, 34–38
networks, and culture, 5–6
Newton, John, 173
New United Motor Manufac-
    turing, 83

Nike, 22

Oberlander, Alfred, 48–50, 64
office-bound staff, 178
openness, and diversity,
    147–149
open-plan workspace, 158–159,
    168–169
organizational change. *See*
    change programs
organizational culture. *See* cor-
    porate culture
organizational structure. *See
    also* alternative work-
    place; corporate culture
    diversity and, 142, 149–152
    informational vs. industrial
        organization and,
        162–163

PeopleSoft, 160
performance. *See also* man-
    agers' expectations; set-
    up-to-fail syndrome
    alternative workplace
        implementation and,
        179–181
    managers' expectations and,
        47–53
    patterns of failure and,
        51–53
    self-fulfilling prophecies
        and, 49–51
performance evaluation
    costs and benefits of inter-
        vention and, 220–222
    effective interventions and,

212–217
encouragement of weak performers and, 217–220
personal values, and compensation, 90, 99
personnel management. *See also* alternative workplace; compensation system; diversity; empowerment; managers' expectations; set-up-to-fail syndrome
productivity and, 47–53
selection of subordinates and, 64
treatment of subordinates and, 53–59
turnover and, 65–67, 78
workforce segmentation and, 177–179
young people and, 59–68
persuasion. *See also* communication
concept of, 228–231, 251–252
credibility and, 231, 232–239
emotional connection and, 246–251
evidence and, 243–246
framing and, 239–243
as process, 255
reasons for failure at, 253–255
research on, 252–253
Philips (Dutch electronics company), 27–29
pilot projects, and alternative

workplace implementation, 175–177
productivity
ability of manager and, 61–63
alternative workplace and, 168, 173
compensation and, 77–78, 83
managers' expectations and, 47–53
"push back," 165
Pygmalion effect. *See* managers' expectations
Pygmalion (Shaw), 46

Quantum, 75–76

Ratekin, Joel W., 181
Reardon, Kathleen, 254
recruiting, 81–82
reengineering, 103
Reeves, Bryon, 239
Reimer, Dennis J., 160, 169
relationships
alternative workplace and, 181
credibility and, 233–234, 235
Rirey, Kevin, 161–162
rituals, 182–183
Roath, Jerome T., 167, 172–173
roles
alternative workplace and, 165
high-solidarity organizations and, 8
Rosenthal, Robert, 51, 59

Ruffo, Monica, 240–242
Russell, David, 184

Sansone, Karen, 179–180, 183
SAS Institute, 78, 81, 89–90, 95
satellite offices, 159
Savastano, Thomas A., Jr., 190
Schaik, Gerard van, 32
self-confidence
  managerial effectiveness
    and, 68–71
  probability of failure and,
    51–53
  in superior managers, 57–59
self-fulfilling prophecies,
    49–51, 200–201
Servicemaster, 81
set-up-to-fail syndrome. *See
  also* managers' expectations
  aspects of, 198–203
  assumptions underlying,
    203–208
  breaking out of, 211–212
  costs of, 208–211
  effective interventions and,
    212–217
  encouragement and,
    217–220
  prevention and, 223–225
  pros and cons of interven-
    tion and, 220–222
shared desk and office arrangements, 158–159, 168–169,
  190–192
Shaw, George Bernard, 46

shutting down, 207–208
SmithKline Beecham, 105–106
sociability
  in communal organizations,
    21–25
  costs and benefits of, 4–6
  defined, 3–4
  distinguished from solidar-
    ity, 8–10
  in fragmented organiza-
    tions, 18–20
  in mercenary organizations,
    15–18
  in networked organizations,
    10–14
  steps for increasing, 30–33
solidarity
  in communal organizations,
    21–25
  costs and benefits of, 6–8
  defined, 4
  distinguished from sociabil-
    ity, 8–10
  in fragmented organiza-
    tions, 18–20
  in mercenary organizations,
    15–18
  in networked organizations,
    10–14
Southwest Airlines, 77–78, 81,
  90, 94
strategy
  diversity and, 133–136
  solidarity and, 7–8
Strusz, Bill, 89
Sweeney, James, 58–59

Tandem Computer, 93
teamwork, 94
    alternative workplace and,
        168–169, 188–189
    set-up-to-fail syndrome and,
        209–210
technology, and alternative
    workplace, 189
telecommuting, 160, 182. *See
    also* alternative work-
    place
Thompson, J. Walter, 22–23
time management, 180–181,
    210
Timmer, Jan D., 27–29
"Torinno Food Company"
    (fictional company
    name), 148–149
training
    alternative workplace and,
        166, 181–183, 188
    management of new hires
        and, 59–63
transaction-cost economics,
    80–81
travel-driven staff, 178
trust
    diversity and, 152
    failure and, 200, 202
    persuasion and, 232–239

Unilever, 34–38

U. S. Army, 160, 169
"University Business School"
    (fictional organization),
    40–42

values. *See* corporate culture;
    mission statement;
    personal values
virtual resources, 191

Wall Street Journal, 79
Wal-Mart, 85, 97
Walters, R. W., Jr., 64
Warner Brothers, 16
Whole Foods Market, 81, 94
work environment. *See also*
    alternative workplace
    prevention of failure and,
        225
    push back and, 165
    turnover and, 89–90
work style
    alternative workplace and,
        180–181
    diversity and, 124–125,
        136–139, 140

Xerox, 89

young employees, and man-
    agers' expectations,
    59–68